EDUCATION FOR CITIZENSHIP IN A MULTICULTURAL SOCIETY

Available in the Cassell Education series:

Education for Citizenship in a Multicultural Society

James Lynch

CASSELL

Cassell
Villiers House   387 Park Avenue South
41/47 Strand   New York
London   NY 10016–8810
WC2N 5JE   USA

British Library Cataloguing-in-Publication Data

Lynch, James, *1936–*
    Education for citizenship in a multicultural society.
    I. Title
    370.115

Library of Congress Cataloging-in-Publication Data

Lynch, James.
    Education for citizenship in a multicultural society / James Lynch.
        p.   cm. — (Cassell education series)
    Includes bibliographical references and index.
    ISBN 0–304–31931–7 — ISBN 0–304–31929–5 (pbk.)
    1. Citizenship—Study and teaching.   2. Intercultural education.
    3. Pluralism (Social sciences) I. Title   II. Series.
    LC1091.L96 1991
    370.11′5—dc20
                                                            91–23924
                                                            CIP

    ISBN 0–304–31931–7 (hardback)
        0–304–31929–5 (paperback)

Typeset by Colset Private Limited, Singapore
Printed and bound in Great Britain by Dotesios Ltd, Trowbridge

The views expressed in this book are those of the author and do not reflect any policy or commitment on the part of the World Bank.

Contents

Introduction

This book continues the tradition of my previous work, in so far as it is concerned with the educational implications of cultural diversity and the role of schools and other educational institutions in combating prejudice. As with my most recent publications, it also sets consideration of those concerns with cultural diversity and the reduction of prejudice within the context of global interdependence and human rights. These foci— prejudice reduction, global interdependence and human rights—are utilized in this volume to illuminate issues of democratic citizenship within culturally diverse communities and societies in a global framework.

CONTEXT AND RATIONALE FOR THE BOOK

The context of world political events in the decade to 1990 provides a rationale for this new departure in the development of education for global citizenship within politically pluralist societies. That decade saw the democratic coming of age of many nations across the globe to such an extent that by the end of 1990 the proportion of countries which could be described as liberal democracies was above 50 per cent of the nations of the world. Most of the newcomers to that democratic club were almost immediately faced with the problem of reconciling the freedoms inherent in democratic pluralism with the challenges of cultural diversity in one form or another. Most of these newer democracies had little or no democratic tradition within living memory and their gossamer-thin institutional commitment was almost immediately subject to the pressures of a multiculturalism whose very existence had long been denied.

The issue was increasingly posed of how education, and more specifically education for citizenship, could assist in developing the values and institutions necessary to sustain culturally pluralist and democratic societies internally and in their relationships with each other and the rest of the world. But older democracies were also faced with the need to reinterpret their often outmoded democratic traditions to attune them to a more modern age of increased cultural diversity combined with a greater global

1

interdependence, which placed on them a heavier onus for the dissemination and sustenance of democratic values and institutions.

From both sets of countries, the old democracies and the new, a growing conviction is arising of democracy being the birthright of all humankind and all nations, rather than the privilege of the few. Thus, the challenge has become not just democracy, but global democracy. The imperative of the 1990s is to share internationally the values of democratic pluralism in a process which will reinforce global interdependence and active membership of a world society. For educators the challenge of the 1990s is to deliver not just education for citizenship of a pluralist democracy, but education for active global democracy, founded on universal values about the nature of human beings and their social behaviour.

In response to that challenge for the 1990s, this book proposes a new multilayered approach to education for democratic citizenship within a local, national and global context of cultural pluralism and growing aspirations for democracy. The book aims to set the parameters for a new approach to education for citizenship which can develop concerned and active participants in local, national and international life, who can critically appraise and judge the merits of domestic, national and international policies against a clarified and reflective system of values, grounded in human rights and social responsibilities. It aims to show how an essentially emancipatory concept of citizenship education,[1] which can address issues of power and hegemony, human rights and social responsibility at local, national and international levels, can be disseminated and developed through the formal school system.

The approach recognizes three **levels** of personal consciousness and social participation: *local*, *national* and *international*. These three levels are seen as interdependent and mutually supportive, comprising an interrelated network of human rights and social responsibilities across all **domains**: *social*, *cultural*, *environmental* and *economic*. Each level and domain is symbiotic with the others. For all practical purposes, for example, the achievement of justice is considered as indivisible across all levels and domains, except for purposes of theoretical analysis. The existence of an 'equally just' national society, based on reciprocity and mutuality, requires a just international society, and just communities are prerequisite to both. There can be no just citizenship of a just national society which ignores equal justice to other societies and communities, through social, cultural or environmental insensitivity, ignorance, exploitation or unequal economic, environmental or political covenants.

In its narrower national definition, the concept of an 'equally just society' has perhaps been best summarized in the work of Rawls under the first priority principle of *equal basic liberties*,[2] a formulation which links inextricably the ideas of freedom and equality as the foundations of the just society, and if of a just society, then also (in the context of this book) the foundations of a just global society, where the equal right of each person to the most extensive system of equal basic liberties consistent with a similar system for all is a fundamental international principle. The concept of a just world society needs to include many of the legal, economic and social 'taken-for-granteds' of the wealthy western democracies. Thus, a just global society has both broader geographical limits and wider domains of activity than exist at the national level; these have been to some extent codified in international instruments, although many national proclamations of justice remain silent about them.

Another aspect of a just global society is sustainable development. This has been defined as 'development which meets the goals of the present without compromising the ability of future generations to meet their own needs'[3] and is regarded in this book as a task not just of trade-offs between economic development and ecological sustainability, but also of human rights and social responsibilities in the relationship between North and South. Global futures are more than economic, they are also focused on human reciprocity, civil rights and social responsibilities.

Schooling for citizenship must, therefore, take account of every level and domain within a global context of human rights and social responsibilities, contributing to the achievement of democratic values and behaviour in pluralist societies and in a culturally diverse world, which cannot be achieved at any one level or in any one domain alone. Schools have a unique and indispensable function in the legitimation of justice within global pluralism and sustainable development as defined above. The three levels of citizenship, for which schools must prepare and which they must seek to embody, are not considered solely as states of occupancy or belonging, but rather as processes of self and social awareness and actualization. It is the task of citizenship education to empower individuals and groups for creative participation in those processes.

The tripartite conceptualization of citizenship at the core of the book, which crosses all four domains, is used to address *cognitive, affective* and *conative* **objectives** in two major international **dimensions**: *human rights* and *social responsibilities*. These levels, domains and objectives are marshalled and focused on the enhancement of the capacity of personnel at *systemic, institutional* and *individual* levels to improve their professional practice, whether as administrators or educators. These overlapping concepts are used, in turn, to suggest educational goals, curricular content and strategies as well as methods of evaluation, materials and professional development strategies to test individual, institutional and systemic achievement of the goals of a process-oriented education for global citizenship. For those goals to be achieved, however, the nature of citizenship education and its place in the school curriculum must be radically reassessed so that schools, teachers and education systems become expressive of the values and assumptions underlying human rights and social responsibility. To avoid needless repetition, the term 'global citizenship education' is used throughout the book to refer to education for citizenship at the three levels (local, national and international). This book is dedicated to the discourse about the achievement of that essentially emancipatory goal.

SUMMARY OF THE CONTENTS OF THE BOOK

In the first chapter, the development of the concepts of citizenship and of education for citizenship is briefly described. A conceptual framework of three levels of citizenship—local, national and international—is introduced. The chapter rehearses the main arguments for and against education for world citizenship and identifies a major weakness in the exclusivity of the debate, in the sense that it generally implies an either/or approach to national citizenship. Particular importance is given to a more critical and emancipatory concept of citizenship education.

In Chapter 2 and building on the tripartite concept of citizenship, material is drawn from a number of precursor traditions; the chapter identifies certain concepts as the basis for a reconceptualization of education for citizenship within a global context. I relate these concepts to basic human values affecting human–human and human–ecosystem interaction and interrelationships. The major freedoms and rights are listed as a springboard to the discussion of the alternative ways in which citizenship education has been traditionally incorporated within the school curriculum. The chapter discusses and develops a series of basic aims for citizenship education, which are themselves derived from the overall goals of education in culturally diverse societies. Educators are invited to consider the appropriateness of these aims for their own professional practice, and to reflect on the way in which their own current curriculum is organized to respond to contemporary requirements for an educated local, national and international citizenry.

The aim of Chapter 3 is to turn the principles of social justice and individual morality, enunciated in Chapter 2 at the systemic, institutional and instructional levels, into effective policies and practices, which will enable individuals to lead personally satisfying lives and become constructive members of local, national and international communities. Education, it is argued, is ideologically and structurally interdependent with other social systems within society, the school exists within a community and at the instructional level, the teacher exists within a community of professionals within and without the school and is subject to influence by pupils and teachers. Recognizing the ideological underpinning of that complexity and interdependence, the chapter aims to answer the question, how the principles described in the previous chapter can be reflectively and iteratively incorporated into education, by and for administrators and educators.

In Chapter 5, I give a rationale for the various components of citizenship education. This chapter seeks to translate the macro policy and process criteria proposed in Chapter 3 to the micro level of the school, the classroom and the curriculum. This has two aspects: firstly, the content of the planned curriculum for global citizenship education and secondly, the process by which the planned curriculum may best be delivered. I have developed a rationale for the various components of citizenship education, which also draws on the overall principles of procedure for the book as a whole. Both school and classroom practice are exemplified and model teaching approaches are identified from practice in a number of different national and international contexts. Finally, an attempt is made to meld the proposals made into the work of the effective schools movement and to identify characteristics for the delivery of good global citizenship education at school, classroom and instructional levels.

Chapter 5 then raises the issue to the mechanisms through which a curriculum for global citizenship education may be monitored and evaluated and how the learning of students may be assessed and judged. In this chapter, I have turned my attention to the assessment of students, the self-appraisal of teachers and the evaluation of programmes and institutional practices for global citizenship education. The chapter commences by relating the discussion of the evaluation of global citizenship education to the literature of evaluation more generally. It continues with a consideration of what factors, either intrinsic or contextual, may inhibit the introduction of programmes of global citizenship education and suggests an overall approach which can maximize the background ideological values and professional theories and beliefs that teachers hold. The pursuit of equal social justice based on the recognition of everyone's human rights is placed at the forefront in the definition of criteria for evaluation and professional judgement, whether about the institution and its goals, teachers' professional performance or the achievement and behaviour of students. I have proposed detailed criteria for evaluation, appraisal and assessment and strategies for dealing humanely with deficits or recalcitrance. Emphasis is placed on the need for human resource development, not least that of the educators, and of the necessity to move from what exists, enlisting the goodwill and professionalism of teachers and the commitment of students and communities.

The chapter concludes with a professional dialogue with the reader, reflective on the chapter and, as it is the concluding chapter of the book, on the book as a whole.

PRINCIPLES OF PROCEDURE FOR THE BOOK

In each of the chapters, I have tried to remain faithful to certain basic principles of procedure. That means that, drawing on the more recent literature reappraising the goals of citizenship education and on developments in contiguous curriculum areas, I expose to critical questioning the goals, policies, processes and practices which are proposed in each part of the book. Those principles of procedure are themselves derived from the overall goals of education for multilevel and democratic citizenship in culturally diverse societies. They are aimed at giving the book a coherence and sharpness of focus, but also at ensuring that it is consistent in what it proposes. They are as follows:

(a) that the book should be essentially international and global in its perspectives;
(b) that it should be attentive both to human rights and to social responsibilities;
(c) that it should be essentially 'emancipatory', in the sense of both making available for challenge the underlying assumptions and purposes of global citizenship education and engaging the reader in a dialogue;
(d) that it should address the three levels of global citizenship education: ethnic or local, national and international;
(e) that it should aim at cognitive, affective and conative outcomes;
(f) that it is flexible enough to comprehend cultural, economic and other social, as well as environmental, domains of human activity and their interaction and interdependence;
(g) that it should recognize and express the provisional, immature and tentative nature of knowledge in this field.

THE CONTRIBUTION OF THIS BOOK TO CITIZENSHIP EDUCATION

This book follows the principles confirmed in the International Convention on the Rights of the Child, adopted by the United Nations General Assembly in November 1989, which became effective after its ratification by the requisite number of countries in September 1990. According to that Convention the education of the child is to be directed to goals which include:

- . . . the development of respect for human rights and fundamental freedoms, and the principle enshrined in the Charter of the United Nations;

- the development of respect for the child's own parents, his or her own cultural identity, language and values, for the national values of the country in which the child is living . . . and for civilizations different from his or her own;
- the preparation of the child for responsible life in a free society, in the spirit of under-standing, peace, tolerance, equality of the sexes, and friendship among peoples . . .;
- the development of respect for the natural environment.[4]

Using these principles and my own principles of procedure, I seek to reconceptualize and broaden what has been called 'the concept of citizenship in a global age'[5] to include both community and global dimensions across all domains of human knowledge: cultural, social, economic, political and environmental. Building on that reconceptualization, I propose a concept of education for democratic citizenship for local, national and global responsibility which is embedded in human rights and a commitment to social responsibilities. The book attempts to release the concept of citizenship education from the intellectual and political bondage of much that has passed historically for citizenship education and to liberate it from the exclusive economic and political interests of nationally and internationally dominant groups. I advocate the need to challenge not only interethnic and other forms of group prejudice, but also 'international' prejudice and even 'hate-education' which threaten common goals, such as peace, human survival and the preservation of a common heritage, whether that heritage is environmental, political, economic or cultural. It is a matter of urgency for education to develop creative and peaceful means of conflict resolution and to teach the next generation to perceive and accept an interest greater than economic or political self-interest.

I recognize that there are many different ways to achieve the goals of 'global citizenship education' while still remaining true to the underlying human values. I have therefore tried to develop a process of dialogue with the reader in the way in which the case is presented and the principles and approaches are described. In articulating its objectives, the book develops through discourse with the reader a common core of expectations for education systems, schools, educators, parents, communities and children, to improve curricula and instructional methods, assessment procedures, organization, resource provision and staff training. It does not seek to define minimum competencies for educators or students, but rather to indicate the standards that should be aimed for. I hope that the book will assist each institution and each educator, individually and in concert, to reconsider their role in educating for local, national and international citizenship, having due regard to their own basic ethics and values, but guided always by the primary considerations of human rights and social responsibilities.

NOTES AND REFERENCES

1. Giroux, H. (1980) 'Critical theory and rationality in citizenship education', *Curriculum Inquiry*, 10(4), 329–66.
2. See Rawls, J. (1971) *A Theory of Justice* (Cambridge, MA: Harvard University Press).
3. World Commission on Environment and Development (1987) *Our Common Future* (Oxford: Oxford University Press).
4. The fact that, in the interests of space, I have abbreviated some of the statements and not

quoted all parts of the document does not indicate a lack of commitment to the others. For the full text, see United Nations (1989) *International Convention on the Rights of the Child* (New York: United Nations).

5. Gross, R.E. and Dynneson, T.L. (1991) *Social Science Perspectives on Citizenship Education* (New York: Teachers' College, Columbia University).

Chapter 1

Rationale for a New Paradigm of Citizenship

INTRODUCTION

The brief introduction to this book has set out the structure and content of each of the chapters and has linked them to the foci of my previous work: cultural diversity, prejudice reduction, global interdependence and human rights. These are the overarching themes which I use to illuminate issues of citizenship, grounded in equal justice, within culturally diverse communities and societies in a global framework. In this chapter, the evolution of the concept of citizenship is briefly portrayed and eight major factors are advanced to form a rationale for the redefinition of what we mean by citizenship. From these factors, I argue the need for an internationalization of the concept of citizenship. The arguments both for and against a broader, more world-oriented concept of citizenship are advanced and weighed; they point to the need for a new paradigm of citizenship, embracing at least three interrelated and interdependent levels: ethnic, national and international. The chapter draws on the work of Rawls for the concept of 'equal justice' and argues that it must apply reciprocally and interdependently at all three levels to apply fully at any.[1] This tripartite definition is then linked to the central, unique and indispensable role of schools and educators in preparing for citizenship.

In this chapter, I want to share with the reader an alternative concept of citizenship to the currently dominant one based on nationality. I do not, however, wish to exclude this latter concept of citizenship from this chapter or this book. Quite the reverse. My aim is to expand the concept of citizenship as currently focused on nationality; I will embrace but go considerably beyond the idea of education for national citizenship to the recognition of the need for education for a multiple-levelled global citizenship. First, the reader and I must agree that citizenship is, in any case, in an evolutionary state and has been so since its conception. My aim is then to argue that there are a number of changes in international affairs which compel us to reassess what we mean both by citizenship and by citizenship education, and to give them both a more global connotation. Not least, I want to make clear that there can be no just citizenship of a just national society which ignores equal justice to other societies and communities, through ignorance, exploitation or unequal economic, environmental or political covenants. From those factors and elements, I aim to draw together the threads of a new paradigm for citizenship and citizenship education. I aim to identify, in outline, the role of educators and schools in the affluent pluralist democracies in the de- and re-construction of the concepts of citizenship and the principles of good citizenship education. En route, I want to emphasize that good citizenship education does not mean less educational effectiveness but more, because it means addressing not just academic or economic objectives, but also political, social and cultural ones. Finally, I want to make it clear that the ideas in this book are provisional and exploratory, and are to be seen as a contribution to the debate about the internationalization of citizenship education.

THE EVOLUTIONARY NATURE OF THE CONCEPT OF CITIZENSHIP

Not without earlier precursors,[2] the concept of education for citizenship has ebbed and flowed since its broader acceptance through the work of Dewey and the birth of the new paradigm of the social studies in the United States some seventy years ago.[3] During the 1960s and 1970s, the issue of education for citizenship was live in North America and in the latter years even experienced something of a revival, but it has since undergone a certain regression in spite of the efforts of such organizations in the United States as the American Political Science Association, the National Council for the Social Studies and the American Bar Association. Notwithstanding that regression, the distinguishing mark of American society has been the extent to which its education system has tackled ethnic diversity to create a durable civic culture from a mixture of different ethnic identities and interests. Building on the concept of voluntary pluralism, it has sought to construct a political culture of 'integrative democracy', which has left to each individual or group the decision as to whether and how to express their ethnic affiliation. In this respect, both its concept of citizenship and its approach to education for citizenship have been markedly different from those of other countries and especially those nations located in the Old World.[4]

More recently citizenship education has been reappraised by immigrant nations such as Canada and Australia, which have needed to politically socialize large numbers of new arrivals of very diverse social and cultural backgrounds and educational levels into the tenets of citizenship within democratic societies.[5] European nations such as France and Germany have, on the other hand, continued an old-established tradition of political or civic education, but without reinterpreting it in the light of their new-found political and cultural pluralism.[6] Others, such as England, where an explicit national commitment to political education or socialization as part of the school curriculum had never previously been sanctioned, perhaps spurred by the development of law-related education, have begun to consider the place of citizenship within a new national structure for the curriculum. Unlike the United States, however, the catalogue of ethnic experience has been too historically slender until recently to make either cultural diversity or global interdependence a major factor to be taken into consideration when defining the rights and responsibilities of democratic citizenship.

To some extent, the conceptualization of citizenship education has been hidebound by the lack of progress in redefining the concept of citizenship. In its simplistic sense, citizenship has continued to be equated with nationality and membership of the nation state. But, looked at historically, that equation was neither the first definition of the term, nor its predominant use until the age of nationalism. In ancient times, it meant precisely what it indicates, namely a resident of a city or city-state or empire as in the case of *civis romanus*. In medieval Europe, not least in German- and Italian-speaking countries, citizenship was belonging to the local city-republic or petty princedom. Only as the age of nationalism developed were people persuaded that the nation was the best guarantor of their hopes, aspirations, identities and security, to be defended against the nationalism of others at all costs. Thus, education for citizenship became at the same time inclusive of the in-nationality and exclusive of the out-nationality: an instrument to forge a homogenized nation-state, hostile to other nationalities and other nation-states.[7] This nationalistic ideology was strongly implanted into individual consciousness and personal identity in the form of values of superiority and even supremicism, but it was carefully circumscribed so as not to interfere with national structures or the economic system.

Of course, such national citizenship was also reinforced by language and cultural policies, which endorsed a national culture transmitted through one accepted language. Language homogeneity was a main policy dimension of the educational strategy of all major European powers from their achievement of unified nationhood, even to the present day, although in somewhat attenuated form. There were of course exceptions, as in Belgium and Switzerland, where other factors at national or local level, such as religion, provided a unifying ideal on which citizenship could be based. These models were, however, never widely emulated, and citizenship in the New World and the Old usually meant a melting-pot approach to enculturation, homogenizing citizens to the ideal of one nation, one language and one people and thus making it more difficult for them to accept the full legitimacy of the national citizenship ideology of others.[8] Certainly, other agencies than education were involved, not least the mass media and churches, where a variety of stereotypes of others was generated, reinforced and disseminated on behalf of the nation-state.

In the period since the end of the Second World War, eight major factors have contributed to a reassessment of the role, objectives, content and process of education for citizenship and a reopening of the debate about the nature of citizenship.

Firstly, there was the evident failure of citizenship education in the Weimar Republic to educate the people to a commitment to the rule of law and democracy. Citizenship education was perverted under a totalitarian regime into an instrument for the destruction of fundamental human rights and freedoms.

Secondly, a process began of defining the rights of citizens beyond the framework of the nation-state and in terms of supranational criteria, thus providing an alternative or enhanced political security for those rights beyond the nation. (An analogous development took place in the achievement of military security through multinational alliances, rather than through single-nation strength.) This process of internationalizing human rights and freedoms, at first through the International Declaration of Human Rights and the establishment of regional and international courts of justice, began the process of making nations themselves, and not just their citizens, accountable for their actions and for the upholding of basic human rights. Most recently, and in contrast with the policies of existing multilateral development banks, which have addressed economic needs and have kept away from 'political' affairs, the European Bank for Reconstruction and Development, founded in 1990, has adopted an integrated approach to development issues, including a concern with both political and economic affairs, aimed at greatly supporting the drive for human rights and democracy.[9]

Thirdly, there was the series of improvements in international communications, which made the transmission of ideas of human rights and freedoms across national boundaries much easier and more effective and, at the same time, ensured that the transgressions of recalcitrant nations were known to all.

Fourthly, and associated with this latter factor, was a more vigorous internationalization of educational endeavour than had occurred under the League of Nations and agencies such as the International Labour Organization or the International Bureau of Education in Geneva. This educational internationalization occurred predominantly through the activities of the United Nations agencies such as UNESCO and UNICEF and later, from the 1970s, through the activities of the World Bank and analogous regional banks.

Fifthly, the improvement of international transport made it possible for large numbers of citizens from one country to travel with ease and speed to make their home and livelihood in another country. The burgeoning economies of Western Europe and North America capitalized on that mobility with their insatiable demands for labour.

Sixthly, and strongly related to this last factor, was the growing internationalization of industry, business and commerce and the growing economic interdependence of nations. Multinational companies were increasingly the order of the day, and more and more it was industries rather than nations that competed globally.[10]

Seventh, and strongly related to the internationalization of commerce and transport, was the internationalization of pollution. There was a 'greening' of world consciousness, and an increasing awareness of the finite nature of the world's resources, of the profligacy of the one-third of the world's population which lived in the North, and of the environmental degradation on land, in the seas and in the atmosphere, which could not be confined to the slate of a single nation, but which had to be carried by all. Associated with this was a new emphasis on attacking population growth as a major cause of poverty and environmental destruction.

Finally and much more recently, with the decline of the East–West military stalemate, the post-war arena of competition shifted more and more to the economic rather than the military domain (not without certain notable exceptions, such as Suez in 1956, Vietnam in the 1970s and Afghanistan in the 1980s). Recently both East and West have been racked by major crises of political legitimation, often deriving from inadequate strategies for dealing with diversity. The search for a new global order to replace the long-standing political bipolarity also led to a growing role for supranational organizations in issues which were previously considered to be the prerogative of individual countries, such as the environment, drug trafficking and terrorism.

These eight factors formed the background for a new debate about citizenship education. But the form and purposes of citizenship education, its aims, content and particularly its processes were also influenced by developments in the field of education and the social and environmental sciences, including theoretical and practical advances in sociology, science, education and the theory and practice of teaching more generally. Of especial interest in the context of this book was the revival of interest in alternative concepts of citizenship, aiming at the development of character, attitudes and values. This reorientation was combined with a greater emphasis on reflexive and active approaches and dynamic processes and on teaching the skills of reflective thinking, citizen decision-making and political participation.[11] Some educators referred to this phenomenon as teaching social actioning, while some nations defined it as education for active citizenship.[12] It is a matter of some interest that newer nations, in contrast, tended to reproduce the traditional passive and cognitive approach.[13]

Then, too, there was the work of the Intergroup Education Movement, the continued tradition of research into prejudice, the burgeoning of the American civil rights movement, the burst of research into ethnicity and race relations in the 1970s and 1980s and the rise of the feminist movement. There was the concern in many pluralist societies with ethnic studies and with what later came to be called multicultural education in most anglophone Western democracies and intercultural education in francophone countries as a potential remedy for the perceived social and educational problems arising from mass immigration. Moreover, post-war developments in international human rights instruments and the more recent development of both human rights education and of law-related education in a number of countries have undoubtedly stimulated a reappraisal of the form and content of citizenship education.

Gradually too, the work of the Frankfurt School on emancipatory education and especially its concern with different forms of rationality became available to the English-speaking world,[14] and two alternative modes of citizenship education evolved; the *political economist* and the *cultural*. The former, emphasizing the roles of schools in the broader political and social context, tended to neglect issues of cultural and social reproduction. It was perhaps best epitomized in the work of Bowles and Gintis.[15] The second, deriving from the work of the Frankfurt School and the 'New Sociology of Education' in Britain in the 1970s, addressed issues of the construction of meaning, social consciousness and ideology, power and domination.[16] This latter advocated engagement with the aims and assumptions of education and the latent meanings and values of teachers, which are the foundations of their taken-for-granted professional consciousness, so as to combat a rationality which oppresses teachers into racism, sexism or elitism. This latter model has been referred to as the emancipatory model of citizenship education and I shall refer to it in greater detail in the next chapter.

Particularly influential was the phenomenon of the shrinking world, which gradually began to raise a whole series of 'green' issues such as the balancing of economic development and environmental protection, including the capacity of ecological systems to sustain humankind's ever-growing appetite for the accumulation of wealth.[17] Educators were forced to recognize their responsibility for a more global perspective in education.[18] Questions began to be asked about the ideological, economic and environmental hegemony of the North over the South and the exploitative nature of that relationship. It became apparent that a new international financial relationship was needed, which could accelerate rather than retard the economic development of the poorer nations through trade and investment and the export of capital. This was widely recognized as an alternative and more humane strategy to the likely continued and accelerated, economically induced mass migration of huge numbers of human beings, struggling to overcome the economic and geographical gap between developed and developing countries.

Indeed, the ever-growing magnitude of environmental problems in recent times has raised fundamental issues of humankind's relationship with the biosphere and lithosphere, including human impact on the physical environment and the environment's impact on the quality and quantity of human life. These issues permeate each of the three levels of citizenship, involving science, technology and social science. Human utilization of materials and interference with natural processes at an ever-accelerating rate presents new and difficult tasks for global education for citizenship, not least in the sense of schooling for responsible environmental stewardship. Increasingly, the utilization of land, water, energy and mineral resources provokes conflicts of equity and human rights locally, nationally, regionally and globally, crossing national frontiers with issues of the right to freedom from other nations' pollution.

In response to these and other scientific and environmental imperatives, there have been a number of international and national developments at system and school levels,[19] which have contributed to a gradually emerging consensus. In 1970, the International Union for the Conservation of Nature convened a meeting on environmental education in schools, followed in 1972 by the United Nations Stockholm Conference. This was followed in 1977 by a definition by UNESCO of the aims of environmental education and the publication in 1980 and 1987 respectively of the World Conservation Strategy and the Brundtland Report, both of which led to an intensification of the debate about humankind's common future and the birth of the 'Green Movement' in the late 1980s. Organizations such as the World Bank have recognized the threat to economic development constituted by environmental degradation, and have developed criteria and strategies to strengthen their research and to address the issue as part of their lending and staff development initiatives and enable them to participate more effectively in the international environmental debate.[20]

At the school level, proposals for new coalitions in the curriculum combining social and environmental concerns began to emerge in a number of countries and contexts in the early 1980s. Reports in the United States proposed the integration of science-technology–society (STS) to prepare students in school for a future citizenship role, which demands the participation of members of democratic societies to deal with science and technology-related societal problems.[21] Experimental studies suggest that preparation for such STS citizenship engagement requires not only the appropriate knowledge and awareness, but also the learning of investigation skills and action strategies,[22] thus overlapping with approaches which would be essential to the delivery of global citizenship education.

Similarly, in the United Kingdom by the early 1970s, environmental education was developing strongly in both primary and secondary schools, as well as in many institutions of teacher education, either under the head of environmental education, conservation studies, outdoor education (including field visits) or urban studies. As part of the introduction of a new national curriculum, consequent on the passage of the 1988 Education Reform Act, and in the context of Britain's first White Paper on environmental issues,[23] education about, for, in and through the environment was introduced as a cross-curricular theme for all pupils in primary and secondary schools.[24] It is of particular note for the theme of this book that these measures on environmental education were being developed at the same time as the so-called Speaker's Commission on Citizenship was sitting and preparing its report.[25] In Australia too, the Hobart

Declaration on Schooling, ratified by the Australian Education Council in 1989, resulted in a survey of the existing society and environment courses in Australia and led to the development of a national curriculum framework for studies of society and the environment.[26] Moreover, in developing countries, as part of the reform of the primary curriculum, associated with the increased international and national commitment to universal primary education from the early 1990s, environmental studies was increasingly recognized as being at the core of the primary curriculum alongside literacy and numeracy.

Global citizenship education can contribute to and draw on the necessary process of 'inter-discipline' discourse between social and environmental domains of human experience and knowledge, both in terms of its content and processes. Nonetheless, it has to be acknowledged that there are still academic problems to be overcome, as well as political ones, before a more intensive academic cooperation can emerge across the levels of citizenship and domains of knowledge identified in this book as essential elements of global citizenship education. Notwithstanding more recent initiatives, for example in sociobiology, there is still a certain ambivalence, perhaps even an unwillingness to consider new paradigms, on the part of competing social science disciplines to absorb environmental issues into their thinking in such a way as to facilitate more active interaction and discourse among nature, society and culture.[27]

Thus, overall the implications of the eight major factors and of the narrower curricular and academic concerns cited above have been only spasmodically and unsystematically carried through into the educational systems of rapidly pluralizing and culturally diversifying societies. True, citizenship education began to embrace a reflective and active approach, and there was increased advocacy of the need for a multilevel concept of citizenship, which could come to terms with issues of social reproduction on national and international scales. But, on the other hand, such developments were often counterpoised by the marked tendencies in industrialized countries towards the ideological oppression of the role of teaching, supported by an increased emphasis on often narrowly cognitive technical standards and superficial calculations of apparent value for money, ordered in terms of inputs rather than learning outcomes. The realization that increasingly citizens of whatever country were civic actors on both broader and narrower than national stages was slow to dawn, but the first lights were emerging.

Meanwhile, insofar as they made any specific attempt to educate for democratic citizenship, nations still resorted to the old cliches and sometimes jingoistic symbols of the nation-states of the nineteenth century: king and country, national interest, linguistic or cultural pride; in other words, narrow national objectives unsuited to the twentieth-century world. Even where such feelings were combined with a commitment to education for democracy, that commitment was restricted within the traditions and literature of a single nation-state and only rarely related to a more global context.[28] Linked to the fostering of feelings of democracy were often strains of national superiority, even supremicism; and these gave rise, as they always have done, to stereotypical perceptions, ethnic and national prejudice, cultural and economic conflict, genocide, holocaust and disastrous war. Often too, in schools, the overall aim was to teach about citizenship rather than to educate through and for it; and citizenship was usually considered to be the prerogative of a particular subject area, and not a part of the whole curriculum, the task of all educators and the whole school.

Even the establishment of organizations dedicated to an international concept of citizenship was of only marginal assistance. They were unable, with all of their laudable efforts, to marshal the support to shift the paradigm of citizenship and citizenship education into the latter years of the twentieth century and the increasingly global realities of human cultural, social, economic and environmental existence,[29] let alone to articulate a new paradigm for citizenship education within the totality of the schooling process. Yet, the process had begun and has gained momentum as participants have come to a closer awareness of the arguments ranged for and against a reformulation of the concept of citizenship and education for it.

THE INTERNATIONALIZATION OF THE DISCUSSION OF CITIZENSHIP

Recently, the influence of broad political developments towards cultural diversity and more widespread democracy have thrust issues of political socialization to the fore. More narrowly, within the education sphere, in discourse surrounding such issues as social studies curricula, multicultural education, human rights education, values education and law-related education, scholars have begun to turn their attention to the world context within which historically citizenship and civic education have developed, and to analyse the pros and cons of a more world-open concept of the word 'citizen'.[30]

Ranged against the idea of world citizenship, and against education for that purpose, are, however, weighty arguments and powerful adversaries, locked into influential self-interest. The attraction and easy assimilation of the concept of nation, particularly where it coincides with other cultural factors such as religion or language, is said to be a compelling, even conclusive, argument. In other words, national citizenship is clear and easy to understand and identify with. Dating as it does from ancient Greek precedents, national citizenship is said to be long-lived and durable, its precision honed through centuries of utilization, international currency, philosophical consideration and analysis. The unique nature of the services offered by the nation and its fundamental role in securing rational legitimation through provision of guaranteed security and material reward are also cited as aspects of national citizenship, for which there is no apparent replacement. In a world, too, where not all nations are committed to democratic practices and values, the state can protect individual freedom and rights in a way which no other structure can, both through the power of national law and the generation of national norms of behaviour.

Moreover, it is sometimes argued, the concept of world citizenship is not only a logical contradiction, but it is also impractical given such enormous international diversity of styles, values and moralities. World cultural diversity is so great as to be a powerful centrifugal force leading to disintegration. Further, world citizenship inevitably means structures and agencies which are ever more distant from the daily lives of ordinary people. Legitimation on an international basis will be an insuperable problem, it is argued, because of the distances involved and the differing motivations which different peoples require, as well as their differing intellectual and national styles.

On the other hand, those advocating a more international concept of citizenship, while recognizing the power of such arguments, counter that the concept of citizenship is neither so ancient nor so hallowed as the advocates of national citizenship and detractors of international citizenship imply in their arguments. National, as opposed to local, citizenship, they argue, only emerged in the age of nationalism, predominantly in the nineteenth century. Since its emergence, the concept has cost the world dearly in war, conflict and national isolation, as well as in policies of homogenization of cultures, which have resulted in the downgrading and elimination of many languages and cultures at a more local level.

Such advocates of world citizenship see an evolutionary development from loyalty to tribe or city-state, through many phases to national and then international citizenship; and they ask whether we really have to choose. Increasingly, the lives of all world citizens are touched at once by environmental peril and economic interdependence. Such interdependence places in question (a) the economic relations and unequal sharing of the world's wealth, a legacy of the age of nationalism and (b) the continuation of the 'manifest destiny' of past political colonialism with the contemporary equivalent, economic colonialism. In any case, it is argued, the world already has regional and international organizations, concerned with political probity, economics and trade, peace, justice, social policy including education, international communications and transportation, human rights and many other fields which are controlled not by national but by international regulation.

Then, too, many citizens of democratic societies are also calling their own countries to the bar of regional or international accountability, as the world gropes towards the idea that citizens should have recourse to supranational courts to redress the infringement of their rights and freedoms by their own state. This is already occurring in areas such as race relations, gender equity and the rights of children and workers. National legislatures are recognizing the jurisdiction of such courts as well as the legislation of regional and international agencies in their own social, economic and cultural legislation. The law of the land is increasingly a law of the world. People who have recourse to these supranational courts are not accused of disloyalty against the state, as they would have been in former times.

Increasingly, too, the concept of single nationality is being overtaken by dual or even multiple national affiliation, and nations no longer see it as a test of national fidelity and reliability that a person discards old loyalties when new ones are acquired. There is also a growing awareness that, at a time of surging competition for the world's scarce and non-renewable economic resources and of growing cross-national radioactive and other pollution, there can be no redemption or rectification in single-nation initiatives. In an age when conflicts are increasingly supranational, deriving from age-old ideologies such as religions, when major conflict between haves and have-nots is growing, no one nation, not even one of the superpowers, is competent to resolve the ideological, economic and environmental pressures facing all travellers on spaceship earth.

Thus, this volume seeks to draw on the evolutionary development of the concept of citizenship from the narrower bounds of familial group or tribe, through the age of the city-state and single-state nationalism to the age of global rights and responsibilities and the internationalization of the lives of all inhabitants of this planet. In concert with more recent publications on the subject,[31] this book argues that we do not have to choose between local and ethnic loyalties, national citizenship and global community. Indeed, unconsciously, we have already chosen not to make that choice and we are well on the way to recognizing three major levels of group affiliation: *local community member-ship*, by which is meant familial, ethnic, community or other cultural and social local groupings, including language, religion and ethnicity but not necessarily linked in the same geographic place at the same time; *national citizenship*, determined by birth or choice, but which may not be an exclusive membership; and *international citizenship*, which draws on the overlapping constellations which members of the world community have in common, regardless of the other two levels.

The message of this book is that these three levels are interdependent, and that for any one of these levels of group membership to be effective, the other levels have to be healthy too. It is the task of education to prepare children for those three levels of consciousness, rights and responsibility, interweaving such preparation simultaneously and interactively, intellectually and experientially through the formal schooling of the child. This book will outline the personal and social skills, knowledge and attitudes that are necessary to achieve such a goal, and which are intrinsically necessary, regardless of a student's cultural background or learning rate. Education for global citizenship has to take into account the needs of individual children as well as the pluralist nature of most societies and of the world. It has to generate the knowledge, skills and insights necessary for creative and active participation, as well as for positive and creative dissent. It has to empower students, intellectually and socially, to make conflict creative and seminal of progress.

THE NEED FOR A NEW INTERNATIONAL PARADIGM OF CITIZENSHIP

There are six factors that form the context for this book's consideration of the three levels of citizenship:

(a) the growth in the number of democratic governments;
(b) the decline in military confrontation between East and West;
(c) the surge in competition for the world's resources;
(d) the recognition of the catastrophic rapidity of environmental decline;
(e) the search for a means to overcome the poverty of the Third World;
(f) the increasing importance of the international role of education in both North and South.

All these factors are framed by a perception of social and political anomie in industrialized societies, caused by disillusion with the formalism of the democratic process, the ideological failure of materialism to adequately legitimate the human condition, major urban crises, drug dependency, child and female abuse, family breakdown, corruption, crime and violence, catastrophic environmental degradation and pollution, as well as a groundswell of interethnic strife and bigotry. Taken together, this pathology demands new approaches to human social and economic development, which can sort the wheat of good policies from the chaff of bad ones on the basis of criteria which do not make the facile assumption that all development is progress or that even where it is progress, development may not have deforming side-effects as well as beneficial ones. The overwhelming power of such factors demands the definition of a new paradigm for citizenship and for education for that citizenship.

With the liberalization of political and economic structures in Eastern Europe and the establishment of many democratic governments to replace previous military dictatorships in Latin America, a sharper focus has developed on the issue of securing democracy through education. The contrast has also sharpened with the continuing lack of economic, political and broader social progress in developing countries. At the same time, international agencies have turned their attention to the growing gap between North and South and the problems of delivering even basic services and human rights to the two-thirds of humankind which lives in Third World countries.

So acute has this problem of development inertia become that the decade of the 1980s is being referred to as the 'lost decade', for Africa at least, and international reports are indicating the way in which the economic crisis of the 1980s has arrested or even reversed earlier progress in human development.[32] Moreover, continuing abuse of human rights, and especially those of women and children, the tendency to one-party states and military coups and dictatorships indicate that in large areas of the earth there is no social, economic or political progress. The world needs an international responsibility for remedying abuses of human rights and for the creation of an international economic, financial, political and cultural climate facilitative of human development.

As the previous bipolar military confrontation between East and West declines, it is gradually being overtaken by a surge in global competition for the world's economic resources, of which Iraq's attack on Kuwait is only one manifestation. Some argue that the world's non-renewable resources are being exhausted with a rapidity that spells disaster for all, unless there can be global agreement on the utilization of the world's natural resources for the good of all humankind. Many of the world environmental crises, ranging from the depredation of the rain forests in Asia, South and North America, international nuclear contamination, pollution of the air, endangered animal and fish species to the well-known phenomenon of the depletion of the ozone layer and global warming, are related to this competition for resources.

The prospect of a peace dividend from disengagement in Europe has been much discussed, and the suggestion has been made that it could be used to alleviate the deadening poverty of most of the Third World's population. In similar vein, some argue that with the 'liberation' of Eastern Europe, attention should now be turned to liberating the developing countries from dictatorship, war and civil strife, corruption, exploitation and poverty, which have been their lot since independence. Others contend that the most valuable progress to the world's poorest nations would be liberalization of trade and of restrictive agricultural policies in the industrialized countries. But many observers point with resigned pessimism to the static state of development indicators, such as enrolments in education, infant mortality and life expectation, and the continuing existence of runaway population explosion, starvation and debilitating poverty in many developing countries.

Yet this need not be so. The World Development Report for 1990 states that a substantial increase in the resources for fighting poverty appears entirely affordable. It is a matter of political commitment and the reassessment of donor's priorities.[33] If the developed world is in earnest in its pursuit of human rights, then it has to provide the means to achieve that goal for developing countries too. Again, as the 1990 World Development Report expresses it, 'effective action to help the poor, involves some costs for the nonpoor in both developed and developing countries.[34]

But the reasons for a new more interdependent and global approach are not solely related to idealism and the growth of worldwide concern for and belief in the equal human rights of all humankind. They also relate to the impact on both developed and developing countries of the continuing and growing economic disparity between North and South. With the population of the poorer countries expanding twice as fast as that of Europe at its height in the nineteenth century, economic inequity, severe poverty, lack of jobs, lack of land and lack of hope for the future are all setting up irresistible pressures for mass migration, facilitated by an increasing ease of international transport. Thus, already the countries of the North are experiencing both legal and illegal migration on an unprecedented scale, a flood which threatens to overwhelm the means of the North to cope through its social and economic systems. In any case, it could be argued that such an economically-stimulated movement can more easily, efficiently and humanely be accommodated by 'trade' rather than aid, by exporting capital using investment in the South to boost incomes and provide jobs, rather than by investing in the North and importing labour, thus stimulating these movements of population.

At the moment, however, industrial nations spend about twenty times as much on military purposes as they do on aid to developing countries. Further, over 1 billion people, more than 20 per cent of the world's population, are existing on less than $1 a day, at the same time as the West is still extracting more in interest payments and capital than it is donating in aid and lending in credits to the Third World. The vast majority of industrialized countries are far from achieving the UN target of 0.7 per cent of the Gross Domestic Product allocated to aid. International reports continue to draw attention to the widespread malnutrition, abuse and premature death which are the lot of Third World women and children,[35] at the same time as industrialized countries continue their profligate use of the world's resources. Similarly, nations ostensibly committed to human rights for their own citizens have more recently demanded almost total deference to the totalitarian religious practices of nations which not only deny religious freedom, but also invoke religion to exclude women from their most elementary rights. And majorities of populations in the rich nations are unaware of the human and environmental cost of their own profligacy or of the artificial territorial and personal limits which they set for the application of human rights.

In order to begin to reverse at least the developmental and educational deficits, international gatherings, such as the 1990 Jomtien Conference on Education for All, have highlighted the importance of basic education for development and formed an international consensus on a framework for action to meet basic learning needs, highlighting the special needs of women and girls. For example, the action framework, agreed by more than 150 nations which participated in the Conference, states that education for women and girls 'should be designed to eliminate the social and cultural barriers, which have discouraged or even excluded women and girls from the benefits of regular education programmes, as well as to promote equal opportunities in all aspects of their lives'.[36] Declarations, however, are unlikely to suffice, for what is required is a change of paradigms for knowledge, attitudes and strategies for development: in short a change of the basic paradigm of human nature, social association, economic development and environmental stewardship.

Education for global citizenship will require a radical change in values, epistemologies, structures and the mechanisms whereby we regulate our interactions as members of local communities, national state and international society.[37] But how can a concept of citizenship, respectful of human rights and drawing on the ethic of a just society, address such issues? The emphatic response of this book is that equal justice means equal international as well as equal intranational justice. It is no longer possible to covet the just society within the confines of the nation-state and to neglect the justice of others or, worse, exploit them. Moreover, that equal justice has to be across the board, social, political, economic and environmental. Thus, the need is for a new concept of citizenship and for a new concept of education to prepare for it. Both have to free themselves from the existing anomie, anonymity and atomistic modes of human association and society which have dominated Western nations since the time of the Enlightenment. What is needed is a concept of political association which can engender humane, cooperative, idealistic and organic modes of human association and inter-action, drawing on the virtues of social, economic and environmental self-restraint, rather than instrumental, competitive, materialistic, atomized and exploitative relation-ships, which drive human beings ever more to a kind of inner immigration into individ-ualistic solitude, unsustainable consumerism and ecological suicide. In short, the need is to retrieve the ethic of 'fraternity', based on the perception of a greater common interest than self-interest.

That greater common interest embraces all domains of human experience, from the economic to the environmental. In essence what is at issue is the paradigm we use to make sense of our social reality and to strive for our own satisfaction and improvement and those of human kind. Is it to be the paradigm of selfish utilitarianism, of individual-istic, rationalistic materialism, which recognizes no higher order morality than self-interest and the most efficient allocation of resources? Or is it to be one which recognizes human beings as deeply normative affective members of social collectivities, sustained by their relationships in community, finding their satisfaction and the human norms for their judgements in caring as much about others as in pursuing their own narrow social or economic self-interest? As Etzioni has argued, we are now in the middle of a paradigm struggle in response to such questions.[38] Which will prevail? The response of this book is that the old individualistic, utilitarian neoclassical paradigm is no longer adequate to the needs of a world with galloping economic, social, cultural and economic problems, and that an alternative community-focused paradigm, which can take account of both individual rights and responsibilities and of different levels of 'community-affiliation' is needed, together with a corresponding shift in the paradigm of the educa-tion which prepares future members of those communities.

Yet such an epistemological revolution has to contend with existing educational paradigms, based on narrow economic self-interest, purposive rational relationships, distance from nature, and rule by technocracy rather than through participation. Far from cherishing a diversity of cultural perceptions, millions of times every school day, pupils and their parents are told that they must unlearn their cultures and adopt the technicist values of Western society. If knowledge internationally and within nations is used to disenfranchise and disempower the practical experience, knowledge and values of those in need, then ignorance, economic decline, environmental degradation, disease and starvation will ensue.[39] Poverty will increase and human injustice will prevail. But that outcome is by no means predetermined, for knowledge can also be used for the cultural reconstruction of the human condition, for social and economic realignment of material conditions and for the rediscovery of ideological and political coalitions which can liberate the human spirit from material and intellectual bondage and which can prevent the destruction of the very environment which is necessary for survival.

THE ROLE OF EDUCATORS AND SCHOOLS IN THE NEW PARADIGM

Education has a unique, fundamental, powerful and heretical role to play in the process of defining a new paradigm for economic, social and cultural nation-building and the internationalization of citizenship, which can at the same time encourage a plurality of communities and greater attentiveness to the environment. Even at a narrowly utilitarian level, the economic returns on educational investment, for example, have been well catalogued over a number of years.[40] More recently, Psacharopoulos has synthesized the many studies on the 'rate of return to education' from different countries and has found that the estimated rates of return are typically more than 10 per cent and that the highest rates of return are on investment on the lowest level of formal education.[41] Yet nations in the developing world continue to invest many thousand times more per capita on higher education of the already privileged than they invest in primary and basic education. Primary education, it appears, has a direct and positive effect, not only on economic development, but also on productivity, as well as on life chances, health and rate of population increase. Yet primary education, the only formal education—perhaps the only education—that a majority of the population will experience in many countries, continues to receive a low priority and status. Further, within all the discussion, little or no attention is paid to the crucial role of the primary school in political socialization and its potential for education for democratic citizenship.

In both Eastern Europe and Latin America, a sharper contrast may have arisen with the continuing lack of economic, political and broader social progress in developing countries. But, for both those groups of countries, the issue of education to sustain the democratic political gains, however slender, is crucial. Most are pluralist in physical, social and cultural composition, so that a diversity of new democratic institutions interlaced with ethnic and broader cultural pluralism requires development, in order to provide the foundation for social progress and economic advance, as well as to establish political reform. For both of those groups of countries, therefore, education fulfils a specific function of nation-building.

International agencies have rightly concentrated their attention on the growing gap between North and South and the problems of ensuring basic services and human rights for Third World countries. Again multilateral aid agencies and donor meetings have begun to speak out against abuses of human rights. Clearly, educational initiatives alone will be insufficient to reverse this situation, but equally without education for international democracy and respect for human rights, progress will be slower and less widespread. Education in democratic and developed countries, as much as in developing democratic and undemocratic societies, needs to be redesigned and liberated from nationalism so as to transmit basic values for creative citizenship at the three levels. Such basic values would include:

(a)   freedom of conscience and religion;
(b)   freedom of association, peaceful assembly and protest;

(c)   freedom of thought, communication and expression;
(d)   freedom of the media, written, oral and visual;
(e)   freedom of individual creativity within the law, including choice of language;
(f)   freedom to choose one's place of work and abode, as well as freedom of entry to and egress from the country of one's birth;
(g)   freedom of active and informed participation in political life at local, national and international levels;
(h)   freedom of appeal to law, local, national and international;
(i)   freedom from starvation and malnutrition;
(j)   freedom from economic and environmental exploitation.

Of course, such core rights and freedoms (the makings of the values of global citizenship education) each have obverse responsibilities attached to them, which require respect for the freedoms of others. Such mutuality and reciprocity is an essential element of valid citizenship, and a more internationally oriented citizenship education must address both sides of that complex and interdependent tandem and the development of appropriate human sensitivity.

But an approach which is faithful to such values does not need to desert all other objectives, and there is no reason why a commitment to global citizenship education, based on human rights, should not strengthen and reinforce the learning objectives of the school. In Chapter 4 of this book, where we look in greater detail at appropriate school and classroom practice, the issue of human association and learning effectiveness features large, for very many nations have so little to invest in education that issues of efficiency and effectiveness are important determinants of policy. What educational approaches are most efficient and cost effective at the classroom and individual levels? We now have an extensive literature in many countries and across a number of years, which together are often referred to as the 'effective schools movement'.[42]

The effective schools movement in the United States and analogous developments elsewhere have indicated which educational inputs are likely to be most influential in stimulating learning, cognitive, affective and behavioural. At the school and classroom level we also have catalogues of approaches which are effective, including their differential effectiveness for cognitive and/or affective objectives respectively. We even have approaches to teaching which have been shown to reduce interethnic conflict and to foster cross-cultural friendship. Often such methods are based on cooperative approaches to teaching and learning, including more democratic, values-oriented methods in which learners take an active part and use their judgement.[43] Often they imply the pre-existence of democratic schools and classrooms.[44] Criteria for this type of approach, adapted to the goals of a more global citizenship education, might include the following:

(a)   a democratic classroom ethos, giving rise to feelings of trust among pupils and between teachers and pupils;
(b)   collaborative and cooperative approaches to help the development of organic social relationships and foster mutuality and moral reciprocity;
(c)   active participation, including simulation, role-playing and varied group composition, as well as social engagement;
(d)   emphasis on character development, which will include skills of conflict resolution;

(e) rational, holistic approaches to knowledge and learning, using methods which appeal to the judgement of the learners;

(f) help for pupils in evolving and clarifying their own value systems, using situations involving value dilemmas;

(g) emphasis on open rather than closed tasks and questions;

(h) multiple approaches, including different media, strategies and locations;

(i) inclusion of pedagogies involving social responsibility and actioning;

(j) high intellectual expectations in both cognitive and affective domains;

(k) explicit commitment to global human rights as the basis for all interaction in the classroom;

(l) linked, supportive assessment methods, oriented to student success.

World organizations, such as the World Bank, have begun to build on the work on effective schools, combining it with the results of work and research from the developing world to identify policies, approaches and inputs which can maximize learning.[45] These world organizations have agreed to give priority for investment credits to six major areas, among which is increasing the participation in education of women and girls, who comprise the majority of the unschooled.[46] (Some regions have declared the 1990s the decade of the girl child.) The World Bank has reviewed its own policy in this field and has placed emphasis on the need for more data on the position of women in development.[47] It has issued recommendations for improving educational effectiveness, including greater emphasis on learning, investment in those inputs which work cost-effectively and the training of teachers.[48]

International organizations, national governments, regional meetings and non-governmental organizations (NGOs) are beginning to provide guidelines for action, accounts of pertinent research, rosters of what seems to work and what the most potent and influential inputs may be, case studies of successful innovations, critical appraisals of national strategies, plans of action. At the institutional level, there are also detailed descriptions of what constitutes an effective school, and an increasing amount of validated data is available of what classroom practices can maximize cognitive, affective and conative learning.[49]

Thus, in both industrialized and developing countries, there is a growing body of literature and middle-range theoretical work on which approaches to education for global citizenship can be based. All point to an important role for education in tackling some of the urgent and most intractable problems facing humankind, not least those associated with sustainable development, environmental conservation, greater economic equity and peaceful conflict resolution. In the North, education must develop the concept of responsible environmental and economic stewardship and consumerism linked to sustainable development, responsible world economic and political co-citizenship and the North's responsibility for the 'shaping and sharing of a new global community', based on human rights, democracy, the rule of law and market principles. In the South, it must provide the human resource development to pull the majority out of the slough of poverty and ignorance and for the generation of income-earning opportunities, the encouragement of entrepreneurship and wealth creation and the building of a citizenship stature to participate fully in the shaping of the new world community.[50] For both, the message is that nations must encourage innovation and competitiveness, coupled with a long-term commitment to technical training, capital investment, new technologies and education.[51]

And indeed, international analyses have now indicated what is effective in overcoming cultural, ideological and material barriers to full enrolment and learning.[52] This focus on the achievement of education for all has, in turn, reasserted the basic right of all the world's citizens, contained in the International Declaration of Human Rights, to education at least at the primary level. The *World Development Report 1990* gives a two-fold strategy for reducing world poverty: efficient labour-intensive growth, and the adequate provision of social services, including primary education, basic health care and family planning.[53]

Deriving its analysis from the experience of the 1980s, and focusing on children, the most vulnerable of the world's poor, UNICEF has proposed strategies for the 1990s, with an increase in aid levels of roughly 50 per cent. (The Western industrialized countries were giving less than 0.5 per cent of their Gross Domestic Product on average, as opposed to the 1960s agreed aid target of 0.7 per cent on average.[54]) Without a new financial order such strategies are likely to founder in the way that 'adjustment' did in the 1980s. Moreover, even apart from the financial considerations, founder they certainly will unless increased attention is given, not just to the education of new populations, but to the education of all populations for wealth creation and for reciprocal social responsibility.

Thus the need is for both industrialized and developing countries to pull together these often abstract statements and to make them effective for all the world's citizens in a way which is consistent with human rights and humankind's responsibility for all its members. It is the argument of this book that education must address social and environmental as well as economic outcomes and must prepare children for future roles of citizen and neighbour as much as producer and consumer. Moreover, if there is to be greater peace and harmony for the children of the world, education has a crucial role in educating for human tolerance and mutuality and away from ethnic and religious hatred.[55]

These factors are crucial to the development of citizenship for local, national and global responsibility, which is released from bondage to the economic, environmental and political interests of nationally and internationally dominant groups and can emphasize community rather than lonely individualism. We must combat not only interethnic prejudice, but also inter-national prejudice, which threatens peace and human survival, and the preservation of a common heritage within the biosphere, whether that heritage is environmental, political, economic or cultural. This book recognizes that there are many ways to achieve successful citizenship education, and therefore the way in which the case is presented is provisional. I use the technique of dialogue with the reader to develop a common core of expectations for education systems, schools, educators, parents, communities and children, to improve curricula and instructional methods, assessment procedures, organization and staff training. This book does not seek to define minimum competencies but to indicate standards to assist each institution and each educator, individually and in concert, to reconsider their roles in educating for local, national and international citizenship.

NOTES AND REFERENCES

1. Rawls, J. (1971) *A Theory of Justice* (Cambridge, MA: Harvard University Press).
2. A very useful overview of the development of citizenship from the time of the Greco-Roman republics to the present is contained in Butts, R. Freeman (1980) *The Revival of Civic Learning: A Rationale for Citizenship Education in American Schools* (Bloomington, IN: Phi Delta Kappa Educational Foundation).
3. Dewey, J. (1916) *Democracy and Education* (New York: The Free Press).
4. A book which reviews the historical and contemporary relationship between diversity and democratic civic culture is Fuchs, L. H. (1990) *The American Kaleidoscope. Race, Ethnicity and the Civic Culture* (Hannover, NH: Wesleyan/University Press of New England).
5. See, for example, the recent publication, McLeod, K. A. (ed.) (1989) *Canada and Citizenship Education* (Toronto: Canadian Education Association); and Parliament of the Commonwealth of Australia, Senate Standing Committee on Employment, Education and Training (1989) *Education for Active Citizenship in Australian Schools and Youth Organizations* (Canberra: Publications Unit, Department of State).
6. An interesting article in this respect is Bruneau, W. A. (1990) 'The new social history and the history of moral education', *Pedagogica Historica*, **26**(1), 7–33.
7. See the interesting account of civic education in the United States in the nineteenth century, Belok, M. V. (1978) 'The instructed citizen: civic education in the United States during the nineteenth century', *Pedagogica Historica*, **18**(2), 257–74.
8. Barth, J. L. and Shermis, S. S. (1980) 'Social studies: the historical perspective', *Journal of Research and Development in Education*, **13**(2), 1–11.
9. Sonenshine, M. (1990) 'Time for a profitable advance on human rights', *The Financial Times*, 21 August.
10. This is the hypothesis in a recent book which argues that while nations provide a supportive home base for globally successful industries, the economic prosperity of a nation in the last resort depends on the international dominance of its industries and commercial enterprises. It is through their ability to offer rising living standards to their citizens that governments legitimate their rule. What happens when they fail can be seen in recent events in East Germany. See Porter, M. E. (1990) *The Competitive Advantage of Nations* (New York: The Free Press).
11. Butts, R. F. (1980) *The Revival of Civic Learning: A Rationale for Citizenship Education in American Schools* (Bloomington, IN: Phi Delta Kappa Educational Foundation).
12. See, for example, Parliament of the Commonwealth of Australia, Senate Standing Committee on Employment, Education and Training (1991) *Active Citizenship Revisited* (Canberra: Publications Unit, Department of the Senate).
13. See Adeyemi, M. B. (1986) 'Nigerian social studies', *Social Studies*, **77**(5), 201–4.
14. Giroux, H. (1980) 'Critical theory and rationality in citizenship Education', *Curriculum Inquiry*, **10**(4), 329–66.
15. Bowles, S. and Gintis, H. (1976) *Schooling in Capitalist America* (New York: Basic Books).
16. Young, M. F. D. (1976) *Knowledge and Control* (London: Collier-Macmillan).
17. See, for example, Brookfield, H. (1988) 'Sustainable development and the environment: a review article', *Journal of Development Studies*, **25**(1), 126–35; and Nijkamp, P. and Soeteman, F. (1988) 'Ecologically sustainable economic development', *International Journal of Social Economics*, **15**(3/4), 88–102.
18. See, for example, Reischauer, E. (1973) *Toward the 21st Century: Education for a Changing World* (New York: Knopf); the report of the Study Commission on Global Education, *The United States Prepares for Its Future: Global Perspectives in Education* (New York: Global Perspectives in Education); and Goodlad, J. I. (1986) 'The learner at the world's center', *Social Education*, **50**, 424–36.
19. National Curriculum Council (1990) *Environmental Education* Curriculum Guidance No. 7 (York: National Curriculum Council).
20. World Bank (1990) *The World Bank and the Environment* First Annual Report (Washington DC: World Bank).

21. National Science Teachers' Association (1982) *Science–Technology–Society: Science Education for the 1980s* (Washington DC: National Science Teachers' Association); and National Council for the Social Studies (1983) 'Guidelines for teaching science-related societal issues', *Social Education*, **47** (April/May), 258–61.
22. See, for example, the article by Rubba, summarizing research in the field of STS teaching. Rubba, P.A. (1990) 'STS education in action: what researchers say to teachers', *Social Education*, **54**(4), 201–3.
23. Her Majesty's Government (1990) *This Common Inheritance* (London: HMSO) contains a chapter on 'Knowledge, education and training'.
24. National Curriculum Council, *Environmental Education*. Curriculum Guidance No. 7 (York, England: National Curriculum Council).
25. Speaker's Commission on Citizenship (1990) *Report: Encouraging Citizenship* (London: HMSO).
26. Quoted in Parliament of the Commonwealth of Australia, Senate Standing Committee on Employment, Education and Training (1991) *Active Citizenship Revisited* (Canberra: Publications Unit, Department of the Senate), p. 9.
27. This point is made in Buttel, F.H. (1986) 'Sociology and the environment: the winding road toward human ecology', *International Social Science Journal*, **38**(3), 337–56.
28. Masemann, V.L. (1989) 'The current status of teaching about citizenship in Canadian elementary and secondary schools', in McLeod, K.A. (ed.) (1989) *Canada and Citizenship Education* (Toronto: Canadian Education Association), pp. 27–52.
29. See, for example, the history of the Council for Education in World Citizenship, set up by the League of Nations Union at the start of the Second World War: Heater, D. (1984) *Peace Through Education* (London: Falmer Press).
30. Heater, D. (1990) *Citizenship. The Civic Ideal in World History, Politics and Education* (London: Longman).
31. See, for example, the concept of multiple citizenship in Heater, D. (1990) *Citizenship. The Civic Ideal in World History, Politics and Education* (London: Longman), pp. 314–47.
32. United Nations Development Program (1990) *Human Development Report 1990* (New York/Oxford: Oxford University Press).
33. World Bank (1990) *Poverty: The World Development Report 1990* (Oxford: Oxford University Press), p. 136.
34. World Bank (1990) *Poverty: The World Development Report 1990* (Oxford: Oxford University Press), p. 143.
35. United Nations Children's Fund (1990) *The State of the World's Children* (New York: UNICEF). Every year almost half a million women die during pregnancy and childbirth; the vast majority in developing countries.
36. World Conference on Education for All (1990) *Meeting Basic Learning Needs: Final Report* (New York: WCEFA), p. 62.
37. An interesting presentation based on the concept of ecological citizenship, which picks up some of the issues in this section, is Ophuls, W. (1980) 'Citizenship and ecological education', *Teachers College Record*, **82**(2), 217–42.
38. Etzioni, A. (1988) *The Moral Dimension: Toward a New Economics* (New York: The Free Press).
39. For a more detailed exposition of this case, see Gran, G. (1986) 'Beyond African famines: whose knowledge matters?', *Alternatives*, **11**(2), 275–96.
40. See, for example, Schultz, G.W. (1961) 'Investment in human capital', *American Economic Review*, **51**, 1–17; and more recently, Bowman, M.J. (1980) 'Education and economic growth: an overview', in King, T. (ed.) (1980) *Education and Income: A Background Study for the World Development Report*. World Bank Working Paper No. 402 (Washington, DC: World Bank), pp. 1–71.
41. Psacharopoulos, G. (1985) 'Returns to education: a further international update and implications', *Journal of Human Resources*, **20**, 584–604.
42. For an up-to-date and detailed overview, see Creemers, B.P.M. and Scheerens, J. (1989) 'Developments in school effectiveness research', *International Journal of Educational Research*, **13**(7), Special Issue.

43. Slavin, R.E. (1985) *Learning to Cooperate; Cooperating to Learn* (New York: Plenum Press).

44. Gutmann, A. (1987) *Democratic Education* (Princeton, NJ: Princeton University Press).

45. Lockheed, M.E. and Verspoor, A.M. (1990) *Improving Primary Education in Developing Countries* (Washington, DC: World Bank).

46. World Bank (1990) *The Dividends of Learning* (Washington, DC: World Bank).

47. World Bank (1990) *Women in Development* (Washington, DC: World Bank).

48. Lockheed, M.E. and Bloch, D. (1990) *Primary Education* (Washington, DC: World Bank).

49. Although much criticized, a publication of the United States Department of Education gives a handy summary of effective measures. See United States Department of Education (1987) *What Works* (Washington, DC). At a more detailed level, there are also research studies such as Mortimore, P., Sammons, P., Stoll, L., Lewis, D. and Ecob, R. (1988) *School Matters* (Wells, Somerset: Open Books).

50. This urgent need for new human resource development policies in the 1990s, their fragility and the reversibility of their effects and potential for deformative influence by causing increased criminality, population displacement, pollution and family breakdown is emphasized in United Nations Development Program (1990) *Human Development Report 1990* (New York/Oxford: Oxford University Press).

51. Porter, Michael E. (1990) *The Competitive Advantage of Nations* (New York: The Free Press).

52. King, E.M. and Hill, M.A. (eds) (1990) *Women's Education in Developing Countries* (Washington, DC: World Bank).

53. World Bank (1990) *Poverty: The World Development Report 1990* (Oxford: Oxford University Press), p. 138.

54. UNICEF (1990) *The World Summit for Children* (New York: UNICEF), p. 33.

55. Smith, A.F. (1991) 'The international perspective', in R.E. Gross and T.L. Dynneson (eds) (1991) *Social Science Perspectives on Citizenship Education* (New York: Teachers' College, Columbia University), pp. 220–34.

Chapter 2

Reflecting and Planning

INTRODUCTION

The aim of this chapter is to engage the reader in dialogue about a less socially atomized, more emancipatory and community-focused concept of education for citizenship. That concept is considered at the three typical levels of local, national and international membership and across the domains of knowledge identified in the Introduction. The goal is to assist teachers to develop their own more clearly articulated concept of education for global citizenship, which will sit well with their own institutional context and professional culture. I also hope to encourage educators to review critically their own underlying assumptions and values, those of their institutions and the systems within which they work. This chapter draws on the point made in Chapter 1 about the need for a paradigm shift in the way we think about human–human and human–ecosystem interdependence. Such a shift has to be towards greater recognition of the strongly normative-affective nature of human beings. If school learning is to support greater human–human and human–environment harmony, underlying principles of a global emancipatory concept of citizenship education are required; there must be universal recognition of basic rights and freedoms, related closely to international instruments on human rights and the concept of a just international society.

The conceptual place of citizenship education within the various domains of the school curriculum, the whole curriculum and the whole school context are considered, and a strategy comprising simultaneously a whole-school approach and a locatable domain in the curriculum is advocated. A list of approaches to citizenship education is introduced from the literature, and these approaches are organized into a three-dimensional paradigm of structural and epistemological approaches and modes of delivery. Subsequently, a set of specific educational goals is used as the basis for global citizenship education. These are further interpreted into sets of exemplary aims for the school and learning outcomes for pupils in terms of understandings, values and attitudes, and skills and behaviours.

The reader is invited to consider his or her present practice and the extent to which it currently follows the suggested principles, and then to construct his or her own ideology of education for global citizenship. Educators are encouraged to consider the principles critically in the context of the school and professional environment, and of the school's curricular policy, but without neglecting the cultural and political context. Factors to be considered would be the (a) traditional place of citizenship within the curriculum, (b) contiguous domains within the existing curriculum, such as law-related education or world studies, which carry some of the same or similar objectives to citizenship education, (c) the existence of local or national guidelines, within which the educator may have to innovate for citizenship, and (d) the existence of local or national organizations which have an interest in the field and on whom the school may draw for support and resources. An inventory of such factors would be an essential prerequisite to the consideration of approaches and strategies for change.

UNDERLYING ASSUMPTIONS AND VALUES

This chapter seeks to define the values which underpin the concept of education for citizenship in multicultural communities and nations in a pluralistic world context and to build on them the principles of a global citizenship education which reaches beyond the revival of civic learning for membership of the nation-state.[1] The basic morality of the pursuit of education for citizenship derives from such instruments as the United Nations Declaration of Human Rights and subsequent international and regional instruments.[2] These instruments have been given added impetus in the 1980s by the commitment of regional organizations such as the Council of Europe to education for human rights,[3] the drive given to human rights education in Canada by the patriation of the Canadian constitution and the endeavours which were made to articulate the rights of children in the International Convention on the Rights of the Child, which came into force in September 1990. Such declarations and instruments have linked together the political education of the next generation, skills in intercultural education and competence and a commitment to international community responsibility. As the Council of Europe has put it:

> The understanding and experience of human rights is an important element of the preparation of all young people for life in a democratic and pluralistic society. It is part of social and political education and it involves intercultural and international understanding.[4]

Underlying those documents are basic moral concepts such as human dignity and justice, liberty and equality, human–human and human–environmental interdependence and mutuality in behaviour and judgement which comprise together the motivating ethic of global citizenship education. On this ethic rest the human rights and freedoms described in those international instruments on human rights which have been adopted by the United Nations, and these same human rights provide the moral and motivating force of education for global citizenship as defined in this book. They represent a blueprint of values for a just global society. In their narrower national connotation, they have perhaps been best summarized in the work of Rawls under the first priority principle of *equal basic liberties*.[5] The advantage of such a formulation is that it links inextricably the ideas of freedom, justice and equality as the cornerstones of the just society. And if the cornerstones of a just society, then so also the cornerstones of a just world society.

Rawls summarizes the basic principle of national citizenship as the equal right of each person to the most extensive system of equal basic liberties consistent with a similar system for all. The basic liberties of the citizen, he sees as political liberty, including the freedoms of speech and assembly; liberty of conscience and freedom of thought; freedom of the person and the right to hold private property; and freedom from seizure and arbitrary arrest as defined by the concept of the rule of law. But the concept of a just world society needs to include many of the taken-for-granteds of some national societies such as the wealthy western democracies. Among the most important of these are:

the right to life and liberty;

the right to the responsible pursuit of economic satisfaction;

freedom of expression and freedom of conscience and religion, culture and language within the law;

the right to associate freely, including peaceful assembly and protest;

freedom of thought, communication and expression;

freedom of the media, written, oral and visual;

freedom of individual creativity within the law, including choice of language;

freedom to choose one's place of work and abode, as well as freedom of entry to and egress from the country of one's birth;

the right of active and informed participation in political life at local, national and international levels;

the right of appeal to law, local, national and international;

freedom from discrimination on the basis of race, gender, religion, ethnicity, age and handicap;

the right to due process of law and to the presumption of innocence until proven guilty;

the right to participate in the choice of one's own government through an agreed process involving universal adult suffrage, to demand accountability of those who govern, and to organize and associate for political purposes;

the right to free education at least at the elementary level;

the right to private property, held responsibly, socially, economically and environmentally.

It is important for students to see the connection between such apparently abstract ideas and their own and other people's behaviour, between the values, assumptions and ideals which people hold, the ethical consequences of those beliefs and the action and decisions which people take. Above all, students must confront the fact that sometimes such systems act as cultural and political barriers; that they divide rather than unite people. This is particularly so of religious ideals, but less so of human rights ideals, which derive from a more generalized context of beliefs. For that reason, students need to become familiar with the major religious and ethical traditions in the world, and to know what are their common features and their points of difference. That implies that students must be equipped to deal rationally with controversial and sometimes highly sensitive issues, where judgements are often to be located between 'goods' rather than between 'good' and 'evil'.

But the whole issue of rationality in citizenship education is fraught with the difficulties associated with a history of the subjugation of such education to inexplicit and often subliminal purposes, including the perpetuation of national and international political and economic hegemony. Recent discussions of citizenship education have, however, tackled issues of power and hegemony, meaning and goals, asking questions such as: whose knowledge is valued and disseminated?—whose interests does it serve?—and what relationship does it have to power, nationally and internationally? How can citizenship education relate to the concept of sustainable development? In what ways can global citizenship education contribute to less purposive rational modes of human interaction and learning, and instead develop greater empathy, harmony, mutuality and reciprocity?

Such an approach exposes and makes explicit the taken-for-granteds of power and the implicit purposes of schooling within the context of political power, as well as the professional consciousness of the teacher which locks that 'folkloric' knowledge into place. In this respect, the work of Giroux, which draws on the work of the Frankfurt School of social philosophy, and particularly the key concepts of emancipatory education and rationality, is central to the concept of citizenship education being advanced within this book.[6] The argument is that citizenship education as currently conceived functions to reproduce social and economic relations worldwide as well as nationally, rather than empowering students and educators to challenge social injustice and inequitable and wasteful economic relations, which are often harmful to the ecology of the planet.

ALTERNATIVE CONCEPTUALIZATIONS OF CITIZENSHIP EDUCATION

Because education for creative and participatory citizenship is so crucial to democratic societies and increasingly also to their ecosystems, it might be expected that each nation would have a coherent and distinctive national style of citizenship education. That is particularly so when one considers the power of the agencies through which civic education is disseminated: the family, the school, the polity and the media. Studies of political socialization in democratic societies indicate, however, that such is far from being the case, and this lack of coherence may be one reason for the erosion of democratic institutions and the growth of anomie from the political process in most western societies. Then again, citizenship education has tended to function as a mode of ideological domination, bringing about acceptance of vast inequities in wealth and power, shaping students to the demands of dominant groups nationally and internationally, and ignoring the current environmental depredation and degradation, rather than enhancing the capacity of learners to reconstruct their communities and societies according to principles of human sensitivity and reciprocity, social justice, wise environmental stewardship and greater economic equity.

Another reason for this worrying situation may be the location and form of civic education within the school curriculum. Unlike such relatively sequential curricular domains as numeracy and literacy, education for citizenship does not have any readily recognized sequence which must be followed, except that dictated by the developmental level of the children. Nor is it a subject in the sense that language and mathematics are, implying a well-defined and coherent body of knowledge, skills and insights, as well as a well-established and even ancient disciplinary tradition, although there is of course a long literary tradition addressing this subject. It lacks the academic consensus which other subjects enjoy with regard to its curriculum, or even its objectives.

For this reason, citizenship education appears in many guises, where it is offered at all. Sometimes it is subordinated to other subjects in the curriculum, particularly to social studies,[7] where it may appear under the heading of democratic understanding and civic values[8] or as a free-standing unit.[9] In other cases, it is seen as the outcome of another subject, where, for example, social studies is seen as the integration of knowledge, skills and values into a framework that is necessary if the individual is to participate responsibly in the school, the community, the nation and the world.[10] It may be presented as a series of imperatives permeating the whole curriculum and each individual subject, sometimes defined in the literature as a cross-curricular theme.[11] This is the case in the United Kingdom, where it is only very recently that it has been considered to be a part of a new national curriculum, but then only as a cross-curricular theme and not as a separate and distinguishable domain of the curriculum.

On the other hand, as in the United States, the more recent popularity of law-related education has raised again the whole issue of the concept of education for citizenship in the school curriculum.[12] In some cases, it is claimed that law-related education is one of the few programmes that not only develops knowledge, attitudes and skills necessary for citizenship but also prevents delinquent behaviour.[13] In some countries, such as the United States, Australia and Canada, citizenship education is a part of the elementary and secondary school curriculum in almost all school boards, although often as a separate unit or subject or commitment within the social studies curriculum.[14] Some states have even included issues of citizenship, considered in a more global context, within their statement of common core of learning, even identifying a number of levels of interaction and responsibility.[15] Alternatively, some writers in the field have identified different approaches to citizenship education, with the focus being on:

(a) *academic disciplines* aimed at teaching facts, concepts and generalizations concerning social phenomena;
(b) *social issues* involving the identification of topical social problems as the means of marshalling study;
(c) *moral development* involving a supported educational 'journey' along a continuum towards a higher plane of moral judgement and functioning;
(d) *community involvement or participation* with the emphasis on learning by doing or by social action rather than abstract concepts;
(e) *critical thinking* including decision-making and problem-solving;
(f) *values education* with an emphasis on clarification and analysis of the underlying assumptions in human actions and social conflicts;
(g) *law-related education* which seeks to clarify and make accessible the role of law in a democratic society;
(h) *school reform* which highlights the influence of the social ethos and structure of the school in the delivery of democratic citizenship values.[16]

Some authors have tried to bring these concepts together and to list them as a twelve-part paradigm of approaches, including disciplinary, jurisprudential, scientific/

thinking, citizen action, social issues, value clarification, moral development, school reform, current events, advocacy, humanistic development, and preparation for global interdependence.[17] Such pantechnicon conceptualizations tend, however, to mix teaching approaches, epistemological structures and ideological orientations. Others, perceiving this problem, have suggested guidelines about how the various approaches to the social studies should be implemented, including that:

(a) the curriculum should be confrontational rather than expository;
(b) the curriculum should be highly selective;
(c) each unit of instruction should be organized around an important social problem;
(d) the curriculum should utilize relatively large quantities of data from a variety of sources.[18]

Drawing on these varying approaches to citizenship education and projecting from them, we can construct a kind of three-dimensional paradigm of existing and potential approaches to the inclusion of citizenship education in the curriculum and life of a school. The three dimensions of that paradigm would be *structural* perspectives, *epistemological* or disciplinary organization and *modes of approach* or teaching learning methods.

According to this typology, the first or *structural* dimension may exist as:

(a) a discrete unit, located within a subject such as social studies or moral education or history;
(b) a permeative commitment within the goals and content of an established subject or domain of the curriculum, such as social studies, global or world studies or law-related education;
(c) a discrete subject within the curriculum, often entitled civic education;
(d) a permeative or cross-curricular theme throughout the whole curriculum;
(e) a permeative element within the life of the school, seen holistically in terms of content, process, policies and procedures.

In the second or *epistemological* dimension, the focus is on the disciplinary organization of citizenship education or the forms of knowledge in which it appears in the school curriculum. This may be as a traditional discipline or it may be as part of a novel hybrid of knowledge. It may even be as a cross-curricular theme. According to the way in which it is perceived, it may appear as:

(a) a field of study illuminated by a restricted range of disciplines such as history, geography, religious education;
(b) a part of an existing hybrid subject such as social studies, global or world studies;
(c) an objective or outcome from (a) and/or (b);
(d) a 'new entrant' discipline to the school curriculum such as law-related education, or global or world studies;
(e) an interdisciplinary endeavour across the curriculum, related to such areas as ethnic or multicultural studies;
(f) a permeative series of principles of procedure for the whole curriculum;
(g) a new interdisciplinary endeavour drawing on several existing disciplines and incorporating newer concerns with gender equity, racial disadvantage and cultural pluralism;

(h)   a series of intellectual gymnastics centring around critical thinking and problem-
solving;
(i)   a series of social exercises intended to give practice in the skills of active citizenship.

The third dimension is the *mode* or teaching/learning methods which are preferred or
implemented by the educator. These modes are powerful socializing media and they are
probably more potent in inculcating values and attitudes than are curricular knowledge
or materials. They express the real underlying purposes of educators and illustrate the
way in which educators seek to deliver the content and form of citizenship education.
That delivery may be by means of:

(a)   an essentially *expository* approach through textbooks and teacher talk;
(b)   an *interactive* mode where pupils and teachers explore dilemmas and conflicts
together;
(c)   a *social actioning* mode which reaches outside the classroom into the school and
community;
(d)   a *simulation* mode which reflects real-life problems in the classroom and through
participation in school democracy;
(e)   a *critical thinking* mode which concentrates on the development of values through
critical intellectual encounters;
(f)   an *activity or project* mode, including the adoption of prisoners of conscience or of
twinning schools in developed countries.

None of these structural or epistemological approaches or modes is by itself entirely
satisfactory. Many are overlapping and incomplete. In some cases, there is a tendency
for the rest of the curriculum and indeed the structure and procedures of the school to
neglect issues of civic morality, commitment and participation. In the whole curriculum
example, for instance, issues of constitutional rights, liberties and ethical values may be
scattered across the whole curriculum like so much chaff before the wind. Each
approach, structural or epistemological, may also neglect the essential behavioural
dimension of citizenship, which demands preparation through experience and not
merely cognitive implanting. Most approaches also tend to neglect the fact that citizenship is learned through the practice of citizenship, at first in school, and later in community and society. For this reason, citizenship education demands a commitment right
through the school, integrated and sequentially expressed and cooperatively planned
and implemented, backed up by specific location within the curriculum and enforced
through criteria and formative principles of procedure, subject to regular review. It is
that approach which is advocated in this book.

Thus, education for a citizenship that is committed to human rights and derives its
ethical or moral core from those human rights, is necessarily a processual endeavour,
addressing cognitive, affective and conative goals for the reconstruction of social relations at local, national and international levels. This work draws strongly on the work of
the American philosopher, Dewey, with its emphasis on problem-solving, political
decision-making and discovery by the child through interaction with the social and
physical environment and the development of understanding and empathy.[19] The
teacher or other educator and child must construct their own reflective system of
humane values within the context of a democratic institution—the school—which is

expressive of a democratic society. This can only be done as a process of reflective inquiry, where the bounds of the exploration are not preset, but are themselves open to critical appraisal.

The momentum of this approach is provided by the contexts of democracy and human rights, justice and responsibilities, from which can be generated the content and the mode of procedure by which it can be brought into the whole curriculum and its many parts. This, in turn, implies that the world of the classroom and school are reconstructed; they are enlarged and enhanced, extended and given reality and context by the community, the society and the global context within which we all live. Opportunities for creative participation and for reflection of the rights and duties of free citizens in free societies towards each other and to those less fortunate are essential elements in this processual approach. Conversely and equally, it means that the attempt to develop an appropriate global citizenship education implies the prior construction of a microcosm of the just world society at which it aims. Once again the two-way interdependence of the levels of citizenship is underlined. Can a non-democratic institution really prepare for democracy? Can a non-just society really prepare for justice?

GOALS FOR EDUCATION IN CULTURALLY DIVERSE SOCIETIES

It is these basic rights and freedoms which inform the aims of education, which in turn embrace the aims of education for citizenship at local, national and international levels. Concern for human rights as a way of life is universal to such an educational philosophy. At the core, its ethic is respect for all persons and their human rights: a realization that human rights are indivisible. Those human rights transcend the social domain and reach into the economic and environmental domains, where decisions need to be fully weighed for their faithfulness to the basic ethic. However imperfectly, such an ethic is embedded within democratic societies and is maintained by the laws of those societies. This is one of the major differences between democratic and non-democratic societies. But, while the aims and ethic may be confined to democratic societies in their practice at the moment, their implications and application transcend those societies and are in that respect global. Their impact is inevitably to set up pressures not only for the just society but also for the just global society.

It is important to note well that education has other aims than those addressed to citizenship. It must address the creative development of the individual and develop the capacity for responsible economic satisfaction. Education for wealth creation is an indispensable part of any education, and without it there will be neither the economic surplus for creative citizenship, nor the political stability for human creativity. Thus, inherent within the above values is a recognition of the need to balance individualism and self-interest with human interdependence and social responsibility, as well as to generate a conviction, growing out of the Age of Enlightenment, that people have the right and capacity to govern themselves and should not be subject to tyranny.

These two convictions lead in democratic societies to systems of checks and balances designed to safeguard the rights and freedoms of individuals, to apportion public and private responsibility, to balance economic liberty and environmental preservation and to secure an equilibrium of continuity and change. Those convictions also lead to such activities as participation, social service, community self-help and philanthropy being encouraged as desirable civic values. Such basic values must permeate any aims for education within democratic, pluralist societies. Indeed, it is only through education that they may be perpetuated. Equally, however, it is important to note that such values are often contested territory, and that even where that is not the case, both students and teachers need to derive and clarify reflectively their own clear, coherent and consistent set of values, and in the case of teachers the rationale for teaching which derives from those values. This is particularly the case for those teachers who carry a special responsibility for citizenship education in the sense in which it is being used in this book, as process equally as much as product. Here there is a lengthy and sophisticated body of literature which deals with the aims and rationales of contiguous subjects in the United States, such as social studies,[20] as well as more recent reappraisals of the overall goals of citizenship education[21] and its role in the creation of democratic and civic identity and action.[22]

Elsewhere, I have proposed goals for education which are attentive to a context of global diversity, human rights and economic, environmental and social responsibility.[23] These overall goals may be considered as master aims at the *systemic*, as opposed to the *institutional* or *individual* levels. They are, thus, the overall goals for education, within which aims for schools and learning objectives for pupils may be articulated. Often such goals are set down by ministries of education, or school boards or state departments of education or local education authorities. Those setting down aims for global citizenship education such as that advocated within this book must recognize that those aims are not 'the whole story'. They are, rather, subject to the overall goals of education in culturally diverse societies, and in turn need to be further articulated into learning objectives for pupils. Those systemic goals hypothesize that any education, which is responsive to the imperatives of human dignity, justice and rights, social responsibility, interdependence and responsiveness and to the full development of the human personality, should seek to:

(a)   develop qualities of empathy with other human beings, and sensitivity to human diversity and similarity, dependence and interdependence;

(b)   foster social literacy, including the intercultural competence to relate creatively to the diversity of human cultures;

(c)   give awareness of the way in which human conflicts arise at the interpersonal, intergroup and international levels; and to develop the ability to resolve conflicts creatively and justly;

(d)   combat prejudice, discrimination and social injustice, wherever they arise;

(e)   inculcate an appreciation of the achievements of all individuals and human groups, and an ambition to build on and extend them;

(f)   achieve the internalization of agreed, reflective moral bases for human behaviour in culturally diverse communities, societies and international contexts;

(g)   develop understanding of human–ecosystem interdependence and of individual, group and national responsibility for creative and accountable custodianship of the environment;

(h)   foster an awareness of human economic interdependence and of the need for responsible pursuit of economic satisfaction;

(i) develop practical skills necessary for responsible roles as individual, family member, citizen, worker and consumer within democratic, culturally diverse human societies;

(j) foster imagination, inquisitiveness and rationality, together with a commitment to apply them to responsible cultural, social, economic and environmental activity.[24]

THE AIMS OF GLOBAL CITIZENSHIP EDUCATION

Clearly, the aims of citizenship education as proposed in this book will expand and extend the aims of existing citizenship education and incorporate those of a number of other contiguous fields, such as global education and law-related education. Many of the working definitions and concepts, such as interdependence, conflict, communication and change will be common to a number of fields. The aims of law-related education, for instance, have been cited as the development of children's competencies— their knowledge, skills, and attitudes—as effective, responsible citizens in a pluralistic, democratic society.[25] A literature review of the most frequently cited characteristics of good citizens included a propensity for considering opinions different from one's own, a tendency to espouse democratic rights for all members of society, an awareness of societal problems and a concern to improve them, a certain degree of skill in critical thinking, and a positive self-image.[26] Butts has drawn up what he calls a 'decalogue of democratic civic values', comprising justice, freedom, equality, diversity, authority, privacy, due process, participation, personal obligation for the public good, and international human rights.[27] It will be clear from the list that there can be no talk of absolutes and that the list is as much marked by the dilemmas between the values as by the clarity of the entitlement, especially when their consideration is raised to the international level.

Above all, it will be apparent from what has been said above that to be most effective the aims of citizenship education have to be forged on the anvil of the master aims of education within democratic, pluralist societies and to take into account the contribution of other areas of newer curricular development in schools. That relationship is not one of subordination, however, but one of formative dialogue, where changing human knowledge and perceptions may emanate from and change either set of aims. Each set of aims must be responsive to the other, so that jointly they foster not only comprehension of what is but the capacity for creative impact on what is to be. Each set of aims will also include the dimensions identified above, addressing all three typical levels of citizenship.

For some, the aims of education in respect of citizenship are simple and straightforward, as in the statement, published by the United States Department of Education in 1990, of national goals for education: 'By the year 2000, every adult American will be literate and will possess the knowledge and skills necessary to compete in a global economy and exercise the rights and responsibilities of citizenship.' For others, the aims of citizenship education are slightly less economically dominated, and may even emphasize the need for participation:

• to establish the importance of positive, participative citizenship and provide the motivation to join in;

- to help pupils to acquire and understand essential information on which to base the development of their skills, values and attitudes towards citizenship.[28]

Some see the principal goal as being the promotion of active civic participation and civic literacy including the exercise of the rights and responsibilities of citizenship in their own country. Such is the case in Australia, where the 'Common and Agreed National Goals for Schooling in Australia', ratified by the Australian Education Council, include: 'To develop knowledge, skills, attitudes and values, which will enable students to participate as active and informed citizens in our democratic Australian society within an international context.'[29] The aim of such provision is to ensure that all students learn to use their minds well and are prepared for responsible citizenship, further learning and productive employment in a modern economy and for effective competition in a global economy.[30] Others see the achievement of such goals as residing in better teaching and additional content in certain subject areas, such as history, even world history.[31]

But there is a further element, which needs to be emphasized in a global concept of citizenship education: global environmental as well as political and economic interdependence. As one guide for integrating global dimensions within the curriculum expresses this essentially ecological task: 'The mission of global education is to produce citizens who are both knowledgeable about the world and possess skills, values and a commitment appropriate for the support of quality, long term survival of human beings.'[32]

The aims of global citizenship education will certainly need to take into account compatible developments in such fields as environmental studies, world studies, law-related education, human rights education and global education. For example, the aims of environmental education as set down by UNESCO in 1977[33] will surely need to be incorporated within or supplemented by global citizenship education:

(a)   to foster clear awareness of and concern about economic, social, political and ecological interdependence in urban and rural areas;
(b)   to provide every person with the attitudes, commitments and skills needed to protect and improve the environment;
(c)   to create new patterns of behaviour of individuals, groups and society as a whole towards the environment.

The aims of law-related education, as set down in a British project in the mid-1980s, also provide insights into the potential aims of global citizenship education, in spite of their concentration on more narrowly national concerns:

(a)   to raise the legal awareness of young people;
(b)   to deal with law-related problems and situations that are relevant to the lives of young people;
(c)   to develop understanding of the role of law in society;
(d)   to develop the skills to discover and use the law in real-life situations;
(e)   to encourage an understanding of and respect for values which underpin the law, including concern for justice, social responsibility and the rights of others.[34]

Then too there is the element of unpredictability and ambiguity in their lives with which students have increasingly to cope, and the need to encourage them to have a less self-centred, atomized social orientation, which can envisage the satisfaction to be had from the recognition of the common good as sometimes having precedence over the personal good. As Becker puts it, global studies and world studies programmes should:

(a) provide learning experiences that give students the ability to view the world as a planet-wide society;
(b) avoid the ethnocentrism common in sharp divisions drawn between the study of 'us and them';
(c) teach the interrelatedness of human beings rather than simply identify uniqueness or differences;
(d) recognize . . . the likelihood of continued change, conflict ambiguity and increasing interdependence.[35]

For, to develop active and participatory citizenship, focused at the three levels of citizenship and drawing on the normative affective paradigm of human nature discussed in Chapter 1 of this book, something more than hand-me-down information and attitudes towards the existing concept of essentially individualistic, utilitarian citizenship is required. True, students need to develop skills in obtaining information, judging its value and reaching sound conclusions based on evidence. They need to learn how to acquire information through different media and senses, to select and organize it, to locate, retrieve and analyse it, and to organize and express it clearly in speech and writing. But they need more. They also need attitudes of citizenship, acquired by experiential and other learning, including the acceptance of responsibility in school. This will enable the individual to make moral and humane judgements and to take actions and behave on the basis of clarified and reflective values of their own, which are congruent with the values, rights and freedoms cited above. Thus students will become effective civic actors and decision-makers, able to cope with and live creatively with the conflicts inherent within all pluralist societies and communities and to engage actively for human justice, rights and freedoms for all in their local communities, in their nation states and globally, across all domains of knowledge, separately and interactively.

This involves the development of the ability to negotiate and to achieve creative compromise in cultural, social, economic and environmental spheres, rather than to receive as a learner or inculcate as a teacher inert, preordained knowledge and values.[36] Therefore there must be effective participation in social change at community, national and international levels to bring them more into line with the values and ideals of human rights and freedoms. Students and teachers alike must develop skills of critical thinking and problem-solving interactive with personal, intergroup and social participation skills essential to pluralist democracy and the creative management of change. This idea embraces some of the dimensions of what has been termed resistance pedagogy, insofar as it encourages the learner to critique society against its own values, and one might add the values of international human rights; it stimulates the learner to imagine alternative economic, political and environmental scenarios, and it encourages the exploration of dilemmas and contradictions, and envisages a process of identification such as that contained in the pedagogy of Paulo Freire.[37] As one group of researchers wrote, based on an examination of citizenship education in ten countries: 'citizens should be capable of exercising the fundamental freedoms which are guaranteed to them, willing to grant these rights to others, and prepared to cope with future social and political events whose character cannot be predicted'.[38]

It is these elements of *reciprocity* and *unpredictability* in a context of rapid change which make it all the more important that students achieve 'autopilot' in terms of their own reflective values and social and moral problem-solving, so that they can engage for freedom, justice, human rights and popular sovereignty at the same time as they recognize their social responsibilities and know how to fulfil them,[39] something which cannot be achieved solely through knowledge or by passive, teacher-centred learning. Such an approach will involve considerations of the school[40] and global environment and natural resources as well as moral problem-solving way beyond what was envisaged by the early pioneers of citizenship education, such as Dewey, namely the definition of a desirable national and international community and the development of capacities to assist in the achievement of global peace and conflict management as well as local and national negotiation for those goals.

Similarly, at the base of global citizenship education, committed to human rights, justice and social responsibility, is the so-called 'rule of law'. While this aspect may be seen as emphasizing the assumption of duties, responsibilities and obligations by young people, it is equally at the very foundation of a free society, for without law, no one is free. Equally many of the competencies to be developed are the same as those on the other side of the coin of citizenship education: human rights. Not least among these competencies are the ability to perceive the dilemmas inherent in many social issues, being critically but constructively responsive to legitimate authority and knowing what rights are and how they can best be secured.[41] The aims of such education have been succinctly set down in a recent British curriculum development initiative as:

(a)   to develop and extend legal awareness among students of all abilities;
(b)   to enable young people to gain a better understanding of law, its nature and role in society, and of legal aspects of their own lives;
(c)   to develop the necessary skills of reasoning, communicating, problem-solving and decision-making which enable young people to act independently and with confidence;
(d)   to encourage an appreciation of the values underpinning the law and to develop a concern for justice, social responsibility and a respect for others.[42]

From these various elements it is possible to establish a set of aims for citizenship, which include the above considerations and also follow the principles of procedure of this book:

(a)   that they should be essentially international and global;
(b)   that they should attend to both human rights and social responsibilities;
(c)   that they should be essentially emancipatory, in that they challenge the underlying assumptions and purposes of citizenship education;
(d)   that they should address the three levels of global citizenship education;
(e)   that they should aim at cognitive, affective and conative outcomes;
(f)   that they cover cultural, economic and other social and environmental domains of human activity and their interaction; and
(g)   that they are provisional, immature and tentative in nature, as is the state of knowledge in this field.

SCHOOL AIMS FOR GLOBAL CITIZENSHIP EDUCATION

Institutional and individual aims must be recognized, as well as the systemic ones cited above. Institutional aims merit particular attention, because effective strategies for the development of global citizenship education may be inhibited or totally frustrated because of the existing organizational structure of the school and its underlying ideological assumptions, both personal and professional.[43] The iterative relationship between the existing structure and its growth to permit change and innovation is an important consideration in any attempt to introduce global citizenship education. Fortunately, however, schools are increasingly making explicit their ideological assumptions and setting down what they see as their aims, which they share in dialogue with pupils, parents and the community. In particular, they are beginning to consider what may be required to construct a 'climate for citizenship' in schools.[44] Such school aims might include the following:

(a)   to provide an ordered environment, which is conducive to the learning and social development of children, which sets high expectations for the behaviour and work of all members of the school community and which engenders a commitment to human rights, excellence, justice and equality;

(b)   to develop in staff and students a respect and concern for others, their opinions and values and an ability to engage in discourse to overcome conflict and to resolve human contradictions and dilemmas;

(c)   to contribute to the children's intellectual, emotional, physical, spiritual and moral development and enable them to achieve their full potential;

(d)   to foster an appreciation of human achievements and excellence in all fields and a desire to achieve similar standards;

(e)   to develop an ethos of trustworthiness, mutuality and human reciprocity in all members of the school community;

(f)   to develop the self-esteem, self-confidence and social responsibility of pupils and a commitment to human rights secured within the practice of pluralist democracy;

(g)   to foster an understanding of the interdependence of humans with their ecosystem and to involve pupils in local measures for environmental conservation;

(h)   to enable pupils to become economically literate and responsible, realizing the interdependence of economic and environmental decisions and of communities and nations;

(i)   to involve pupils in preparation for active citizenship in their communities, their nation and the world and to develop in them appropriate skills and expertise.

Such an exemplary set of aims for an individual school needs to be seen in the context of systemic master aims for education in culturally diverse societies. In turn, while such systemic and institutional aims are useful as indicators of the general direction in which an institution is moving and also as the basis for institutional dialogue within the school and with its community, they need to be further articulated so that they can express the details of what the school will incorporate into its curriculum and what its teaching methods, processes and procedures will be. They can also form the agenda for discussions about the school structure and organization.

LEARNING OUTCOMES FOR PUPILS IN GLOBAL CITIZENSHIP EDUCATION

In his book, *A Place Called School*, Goodlad proposed four domains for goals for schools in the United States: *academic*, *vocational*, *social* and *personal*,[45] which fit fairly well with the literature on the outcomes of citizenship education in its traditional sense. These domains may be useful in providing us with the next stage of individual development for citizenship education. For example, the purpose statement for global education published by the National Council for the Social Studies also envisages four major areas of knowledge, abilities, valuing and social participation. Under the social, Becker has grouped civic and cultural goals, which he further subdivided into interpersonal understandings, citizenship participation, enculturation and moral and ethical character. If we take this domain as representing one nexus of goals for schools seeking to educate for citizenship in pluralist societies, but accept that there is overlap and interdependence with the other goal domains, we may devise a set of working objectives which may help to guide our search for a citizenship education which permeates the very being of a school. Under that goal we may envisage objectives of *understandings*, *values and attitudes* and of *skills and behaviours*.

Understandings

of the similarities and differences of human beings, their values, locations and styles of social and political life and the influence of these on individuals, groups, societies and the world community;
of economic and environmental interdependence at local, national and international levels;
of the varying ways in which pluralist democracies work;
of the major human rights and responsibilities at the three levels and in social, cultural, economic and environmental spheres;
of the varying ways in which pluralist democracies function;

Values and attitudes

commitment to the values of human rights and pluralist democracy;
reciprocity, empathy and mutuality in all human affairs, whether cultural, social, economic, political or environmental;
willingness to participate in civic life at appropriate levels;
attitudes of openness to the cultures and ideas of others and mutuality in human relations;
a strong commitment to gender and racial equality and willingness to fight socially and politically for them;
a commitment to persuasion and dialogue as the major means to achieve social justice and change;
awareness of gender, cultural and national stereotyping and bias in their own culture and language and commitment to overcome them.

Skills and behaviours

autonomous but socially responsible moral judgement and integrity, based on reflective and clarified values;

ability to accept the provisionality of human social and moral knowledge and the uncertainty which this implies;

responsible consumer and producer skills, responsive to the human and environmental rights of others;

engagement for human rights, justice and dignity;

ability to evaluate the economic, social, political and environmental decisions of others objectively;

interpersonal competence and the ability to make and maintain good human relationships;

ability to sustain dialogue within and across cultures;

communicative competence across a range of media and registers of language;

political literacy including the capacity for creative dissent, problem-solving, advocacy and creative conflict resolution;

decision-making, participatory and collaborative competencies;

capacity for the development of satisfying and interactive human relations in different cultural contexts and across professional, personal and civic domains.

Needless to say, such learning outcomes, and the preceding aims and goals, can only be achieved by the process of participation by the learners in their own education. Only in this way will the students utilize school learning in everyday life and interaction in school, outside school and in the adult 'afterlife' beyond school.

PROCEDURES FOR IMPLEMENTING CITIZENSHIP EDUCATION

Of course, such goals, aims and to some extent the learning outcomes are at a high level of abstraction and do not tell us directly what to do in school and classroom. Moreover, however much they have been derived from the literature, they cannot be universally applicable. They are a useful yardstick against which we can measure our own institution and professional practice; but such an examination needs to be iterative in the sense that it is not a one-way process, a determination from the goals, aims and learning outcomes. Rather the goals, aims and learning outcomes will themselves be refined and amended in interaction with the individual school, its community, pupils and teachers. From that process, schools and teachers will develop their own guiding principles. Indeed it is important that they do so and make them their own, or commitment to them and understanding of them is not likely to be very deep or implementation very effective. For that purpose of developing individual and institutional 'ownership', it might be useful to begin by asking certain questions. These might include:

To what extent does the school, as currently organized, enable students to fulfil their own full potential, intellectual, social and cultural, and to assist others to do likewise?

In what ways is the school currently a microcosm of 'the just society'?

How far are students able to develop critical distance from their own experience and from their school?

Are students encouraged to clarify their own value system, rather than being given a hand-me-down one prepacked by the school?

Does the normal school routine include opportunities for students to question and challenge the decisions of their peers and teachers?

Are students encouraged to accept responsibility for their immediate and wider environment and the ecosystem?

Are students aware of their economic responsibility to others at home and abroad who are less well-off than they are?

Can students practise the skills of the peaceful resolution of conflict according to democratic principles of persuasion and discourse?

Is the curriculum organized according to the principles of human rights?

Are the modes of communication and interaction in the school non-sexist, non-racist and culturally unbiased?

Are students empowered to take responsible social action and to participate in political life at an appropriate level?

Such questions raise the issue of the quality of citizenship education in classroom and school as part of the daily experience of each student and member of staff. They need to be developed into critical principles which will guide the implementation of the goals, aims and learning outcomes spelled out above. That process will quite naturally vary from school to school and to some extent from classroom to classroom and teacher to teacher, although the fundamental principles will remain constant.

DISCOURSE ON CITIZENSHIP EDUCATION

In accord with the principles of procedure set down in the Introduction for the inter-action between writer and readers, and because no school ever starts the process of curricular revision with a tabula rasa, and further because teachers as much as students need to construct their own rationale and goals for global citizenship education, this section seeks to develop a set of reflexive questions about the base from which any change must commence. It does this by posing a series of questions to which different teachers and institutions may be expected to respond differently.

Are you or your school already implementing any of the objectives and goals described above?

How far do you consider that the aims and objectives presented and advocated in this chapter are faithful to the principles of procedure introduced in the Introduction to this book? In what ways do they need to be changed to harmonize more closely?

Does the case for different levels of citizenship, for which schools must prepare, seem reasonable to you in the context of your own school and the background of your students?

Are there any preexisting commitments to citizenship education, however defined, in the existing curriculum of your school?

Are there any subjects or cross-curricular themes such as law-related education, multicultural education or global studies in your school or district?

Do any of your colleagues already deal with issues of citizenship education under the heading of a subject such as moral education, for example?

Are any of your colleagues interested in citizenship education and could you form a study group?

Do local or national documents require the teaching of citizenship education, and if so, in what form and with what goals?

How can you incorporate concerns with global citizenship in your own curriculum and teaching?

If it does not already exist, how can you begin the process of achieving a school policy statement on citizenship education?

Would the introduction of citizenship education have implications for the material and textbooks, exemplars and teaching methods and assessment which you currently use?

How might the introduction of citizenship education affect relationships with colleagues, students and the community?

What additional training will you need? How can you obtain it?

From such questions, a plan for the implementation of global citizenship education in individual schools and classrooms emerges for individual educators and their colleagues, which will carry the dialogue of this book across the field of discussion of goals, aims and learning outcomes into the discussion of policies and practices. Only in that way can global citizenship education be a part of the reflective professional biography of each teacher and each school. It is that transition from principles into policies and processes which is the focus of the next chapter.

NOTES AND REFERENCES

1. Butts, R.F. (1980) *The Revival of Civic Learning. A Rationale for Citizenship Education in American Schools.* (Bloomington, IN: The Phi Delta Kappa Educational Foundation).
2. Selby, D. (1987) *Human Rights* (Cambridge; Cambridge University Press).
3. Starkey, H. (1988) 'Human rights: the values for world studies and multicultural education', *Westminster Studies in Education*, **9**, 57–66.
4. Council of Europe (1985) *Committee of Ministers, Recommendation No. (85) 7 of the Committee of Ministers to Member States on Teaching and Learning about Human Rights in Schools* (Strasbourg: Council of Europe).
5. See Rawls, J. (1971) *A Theory of Justice* (Cambridge, MA.: Harvard University Press).
6. Giroux, H. (1980) 'Critical theory and citizenship education', *Curriculum Inquiry*, **10**(4), 329–66.
7. See the survey of ways of teaching about citizenship in Canadian schools, Masemann, V.L. (1989) 'The current status of teaching about citizenship in Canadian elementary and secondary schools', in McLeod, K.A. (1989) *Canada and Citizenship Education* (Toronto: Canadian Education Association), pp. 27–52.
8. California State Department of Education (1988) *History–Social Science Framework* (Sacramento, CA: California State Board of Education), p. 11.
9. See, for example, Arizona Department of Education (1989) *Arizona Social Studies Essential Skills* (Phoenix, AZ: Arizona Department of Education), p. 7.
10. New Jersey Department of Education, Division of General Academic Education (1988) *World Histories/Cultures Curriculum Guidelines* (Trenton, NJ: New Jersey State Department of Education), p. 1.

11. See, for example, in the new English national curriculum, National Curriculum Council (1990) *The Whole Curriculum*, Curriculum Guidance Series No. 3. (York: National Curriculum Council).

12. Schools Curriculum Development Committee (1987) *Curriculum at the Crossroads* (London: Schools Curriculum Development Committee/Law Society).

13. See Iowa Center for Law-Related Education, 'LRE in Iowa: past achievements and future goals', *LRE Perspectives*, 1(1), 1.

14. See, for example, Bank, J.A. (1989) 'Social science knowledge and citizenship education', paper presented at the National Center for Research on Teacher Education, Policy Seminar on the Knowledge Growth of Beginning Teachers, Washington, DC 24–5 February; and Kennedy, K.J. (1990) 'Social science education as the context for parliamentary education and the promotion of active citizenship', *Citizenship Educator*, 1(1), 1–9.

15. Maine Department of Educational and Cultural Services (1990) *Maine's Common Core of Learning* (Augusta, ME), p. 20.

16. The above list is adapted from the report of The National Task Force on Citizenship Education (1977) *Education for Responsible Citizenship* (New York: McGraw-Hill), quoted in Butts, R.F. (1980) *The Revival of Civic Learning. A Rationale for Citizenship Education in American Schools* (Bloomington, IN: Phi Delta Kappa Educational Foundation), 100–4 and *passim*, and more recent work by Dynneson and Gross: see Dynneson, T.L. and Gross, R.E. (1991) 'The educational perspective: citizenship education in American society', in R.E. Gross and T.L. Dynneson (eds), *Social Science Perspectives on Citizenship Education* (New York: Teachers' College, Columbia University).

17. Dynneson, T.L. and Gross, R.E. (1991) 'The educational perspective: citizenship education in American society', in R.E. Gross and T.L. Dynneson (eds), *Social Science Perspectives on Citizenship Education* (New York: Teachers' College, Columbia University).

18. Engle, S.H. and Ochoa, A. (1986) 'A curriculum for democratic citizenship', *Social Education*, November/December, 514–25.

19. Dewey, J. (1916) *Democracy and Education* (New York: The Free Press).

20. See, for example, Engle, S.H. and Ochoa, A.S. (1988) *Education for Democratic Citizenship: Decision-Making in the Social Studies* (New York: Teachers' College Press); Hunt, M.P. and Metcalf, L.E. (1955) *Teaching High School Social Studies: Problems in Reflective Thinking and Social Understanding* (New York: Harper & Row); Newman, F.M. (1975) *Education for Citizenship Action: Challenge for the Secondary Curriculum* (Berkeley, CA: McCutchan); and Shaver, J.P. (ed.) (1977) *Building Rationales for Citizenship Education*. Bulletin 52. (Washington, DC: National Council for the Social Studies).

21. See Butts , R.F. (1988) *The Morality of Democratic Citizenship: Goals for Civic Education in The Republic's Third Century* (Calabasas, CA: Center for Civil Education).

22. Janowitz, M. (1983) *The Reconstruction of Patriotism: Education for Civic Consciousness* (Chicago; University of Chicago Press).

23. Lynch, J. (1989) *Multicultural Education in a Global Society* (London: Falmer Press), pp. xvii–xviii.

24. I have slightly altered the aims set down in the original text for two reasons. Firstly, my own thinking has progressed since I wrote the original set some three years ago (see Lynch, J. (1989) *Multicultural Education in a Global Society* (London: Falmer Press)). And, secondly, the focus of my writing on this occasion is citizenship within a context of cultural diversity. The overall thrust and the bulk of the details remain the same.

25. Anderson, C.C. (1980) 'Promoting responsible citizenship through elementary law-related education', *Social Education*, **44** (May), 383–86.

26. Curtis, C.K. (1983) 'Relationships among certain citizenship variables', *Journal of Social Studies Research*, 7(2), 18–28.

27. Butts, R.F. (1980) *The Revival of Civic Learning: A Rationale for Citizenship Education in American Schools* (Bloomington, IN: Phi Delta Kappa Educational Foundation), pp. 121–67.

28. National Curriculum Council, *The Whole Curriculum* (York) repeated and elucidated in National Curriculum Council (1990) *Education for Citizenship*, Curriculum Guidance Series No. 8 (York: National Curriculum Council).

29. Quoted in Parliament of the Commonwealth of Australia, Senate Standing Committee on Employment, Education and Training (1991) *Active Citizenship Revisited* (Canberra; Publications Unit, Department of the Senate), p. 9.

30. This is a paraphrase of the major goals of a new citizenship package in the United States, called CIVITAS, which appeared in 1991.

31. See, for example, the 'Education for Democracy Project' in the United States: Gagnon, P. (1989) *Democracy's Half Told Story. What American History Textbooks Should Add* (Washington DC: American Federation of Teachers); and Gagnon, P. (1987) *Democracy's Untold Story. What World History Textbooks Neglect* (Washington, DC: American Federation of Teachers).

32. Iowa Department of Education (1989) *A Guide for Integrating Global Education across the Curriculum* (Des Moines, IA: State of Iowa), p. 7.

33. United Nations Scientific, Social and Cultural Organization (1977) *Trends in Environmental Education* (Paris: UNESCO), and (1977) *Needs and Priorities in Environmental Education: An International Survey* (Paris: UNESCO).

34. Schools Curriculum Development Committee (1987) *Curriculum at the Crossroads* (London: Schools Curriculum Development Committee/Law Society).

35. Becker, J. (1979) *Schooling for a Global Age* (New York: McGraw-Hill).

36. For more details of the kind of specific skills needed for creative citizenship, see Remy, R.C. (1980) *Handbook of Basic Citizenship Competencies* (Alexandria, VA: Association for Supervision and Curriculum Development).

37. Freire, P. (1973) *Education for Critical Consciousness* (New York: Seabury Press).

38. Torney, J.V., Oppenheim, A.N. and Farnen, R.F. (1975) *Civic Education in Ten Countries* (New York: John Wiley), p. 23.

39. See the recommendations of the task force on civic education: National Task Force on Citizenship Education (1977) *Recommendations for Strengthening Civic Education* (Washington DC).

40. It is interesting to note the emphasis placed on an appropriate concern for the school environment and its relationship to disciplinary problems in schools. See Department of Education and Science and the Welsh Office (1989) *Discipline in Schools*. Report of the Committee of Enquiry Chaired by Lord Elton (London: HMSO).

41. Anderson, C.C. (1980) 'Promoting responsible citizenship through elementary law-related education', *Social Education*, **44**(5), 383–6.

42. Schools Curriculum Development Committee/Law Society (1989) *Understand the Law: An SCDC/Law Society Project* (London: Schools Curriculum Development Committee/Law Society).

43. Carter, T.L. (1988) 'Application of organization development theory to improve citizenship education', unpublished Doctor of Education dissertation, University of Seattle.

44. McGowan, T.M. *et al.* (1986) 'Generating an elementary school climate for citizenship', *Contemporary Education*, **58**(1), 25–9.

45. Goodlad, J.I. (1984) *A Place Called School: Prospects for the Future* (New York: McGraw-Hill).

Chapter 3

Principles into Policies and Processes

INTRODUCTION

In Chapter 2, building on the tripartite concept of citizenship outlined in Chapter 1, I sought to share with the reader some of the underlying assumptions and values which underpin the concept and practice of education for global citizenship, which is being advanced in this book. Drawing upon the conceptualization introduced at the end of Chapter 2, this third chapter proposes principles of procedure related to the structure, processes and content of global citizenship education for the achievement of cognitive, affective and conative objectives for a 'civic' curriculum. Policy guidelines at international, national and institutional levels are generated and listed as a preparation for the more detailed curriculum content to be introduced in Chapter 4. The basic ethic of 'equal justice', understood as applying to all peoples internationally, is repeated and, once again, the reader is engaged in an iterative process, which encourages him or her to reflect on the identified curriculum and consider how the proposals may be used to improve the professional service offered by institutions and individual educators. The major concern of this chapter is to clarify the values, knowledge and skills on which a new practice for citizenship may be constructed, and through which it may be continually and formatively monitored and evaluated.

The overall aim of this chapter is to turn the principles of social justice and individual morality, enunciated in Chapter 2 at the systemic, institutional and instructional levels, into practical policies for educators, so that they can deliver an education which will enable individuals to lead personally satisfying lives and become constructive members of local, national and international communities. Each of these levels is envisaged as being cocooned within other systems, where prevailing and countervailing forces are in conflict about the values and purposes of education, but where there can be general, if not universal, agreement on certain basic human rights and freedoms. Thus, education is ideologically and structurally interdependent with other social systems within society and globally: the school exists within a community, and the teacher exists within a community of professionals within and without the school and is subject to influence by pupils and teachers. These different levels and complexities do not mean, however, that the search for universal principles for citizenship education is forlorn.

Given the ideological basis of that complexity, how can the principles described in the previous chapter be reflectively and iteratively incorporated into the policy and practice of education, by and for administrators and educators? This is a particularly important question if an emancipatory approach to global citizenship education is to be developed. This chapter seeks to define the measures which go towards good citizenship education and hence good democratic citizenship, attentive to human rights and justice, social responsibilities and human mutuality at local, national and global levels. Its focus is on policies for structures, processes and content, and their underlying ideologies, not least because even enterprising and creative measures for citizenship education may fail because of not taking into account sufficiently the existing structure and ethos of the school.[1]

TOWARDS A MISSION STATEMENT FOR GLOBAL CITIZENSHIP EDUCATION

This is not to suggest that the social design and cultural values of schools are unchanging or unchangeable. Quite the reverse, for just as schools in different societies and at different historical times have had varying structures and goals, so also the organization and institutional culture of contemporary schools can be changed. The point is that incongruity of messages between education for citizenship and the structure, daily inter-actions and ambience of the school and the behaviour of its members can actually diminish the effectiveness of citizenship education, or worse, it may provide negative messages.[2] Where the environment for learning is teacher-centred and authoritarian, content is either non-controversial or outcome-determined, the school is unlikely to be effective in delivering education for citizenship. Where the atmosphere of the school is supportive of prejudiced or stereotypical views of minority groups or other cultures and nations, the school is not likely to be successful in achieving education for global citizenship, however inquiry-centred its curriculum statement may assert its methodology to be.

There must be a holistic approach to global citizenship education, with a systemic and institutional statement of mission, with which all concur, providing the foundation for individual and institutional values and behaviour, and making congruent the formal, hidden and societal curricula.[3] Wherever possible, such an approach should draw on the real-life experience of the age-group concerned, as was attempted in the 'Educating for Citizenship' programme for the elementary grades in the United States.[4] Schools transmit values, whether that is made explicit or not. As Parker points out, however, the conscious teaching of appropriate and reflected values is preferable to the involuntary transmission of inappropriate values.[5]

The overall strategy of this chapter draws on the *knowledge, skills, attitudes* and *values* derived from the literature on citizenship education. Under *knowledge*, students need to learn in a way that is phased and consistent with their developmental stage and interests about the nature of human association and community and the norm-based way in which such relationships are regulated. Similarly, they need to develop *skills* of communicative competence comprising (a) literacy, including an ability in the field of advocacy, mediation and the promotion of causes; (b) numeracy; (c) bridging those two areas, skills of computer literacy and information technology, embracing the acquisition and processing of information; (d) problem-solving and decision-making skills, based on critical and reflective judgement; and (e) personal and social skills, including skills of cooperative working and human sensitivity. Under *attitudes*, students should be enabled to develop a respect for persons, for reciprocity and justice in human relations and for the rule of law; a commitment to democratic processes, including the process of rational discourse and peaceful conflict resolution; a conviction of the core importance of human rights in human relations at interpersonal, community, national and international levels; an appreciation of their moral stewardship of their environment and natural resources; a commitment to social responsibility in family, peer group, community, national and international relationships; moral autonomy in decision-making, which yet takes human rights as the ethical basis of those decisions and judgements; and responsible economic conduct, as both producer and consumer. Under *values*, it is important that students understand that no worthwhile human society can prevail against an 'anything-goes' value system. There are certain values on which educators and schools cannot remain neutral and they must make that clear in their statements and their 'demonstration', that is in their processes, structures, procedures and judgements. These values are: the value of human life; human rights; social justice and the 'equally just society', as the yardsticks for decisions and judgements; democratic discourse and peaceful conflict resolution; a sense of responsibility for other human beings and for the environment. These are all indispensable value foundations for a democratic society, committed to human rights and social responsibility for itself and other societies.[6]

Such an approach, spreading across the four areas outlined above, must recognize that education draws on diverse, deep-rooted, sometimes subliminal ideological premises, concerning the nature of human beings and society, including social and economic activity, about learning and learners, with regard to knowledge and its worth. Citizenship itself has varied over time and across space in different countries,[7] and it has varied in the form in which it has been delivered.[8] Equally, citizenship education as currently conceived expresses prior values and assertions, so that its form and content may be envisaged as part of the struggle for democracy, as it is successively reinterpreted from one generation to another and from one society to another.[9] Certainly, there is no one paradigm of citizenship education, just as there is no one overall set of values transmitted by schools. As a comparative study of values education in seven industrialized countries confirmed:

(a) no educational institution can be value-neutral;
(b) countries differ in the values which characterize their political cultures and in the values which are taught in school;
(c) no country has had a uniformly high level of success in transmitting civic values;
(d) the learning of values is strongly influenced by factors outside the school's control;
(e) educational policy has been somewhat effective in bringing about desired changes in values;

(f)   the learning of values in school is not limited to mandated programmes of moral and civic education;

(g)   several nations have developed curricular goals to deliver common core values;

(h)   television and other mass media have an important and often negative effect on young people's values.[10]

Notwithstanding the findings of that research, it is clear that countries increasingly have a common baseline of values as represented in international human rights instruments. There is no reason why these values should not be recognized as the values of education systems throughout the world. Global citizenship education, as proposed in this book, will also similarly express philosophical theories about humankind.[11] Equally, it is evident that differing philosophies underlie the varying ways of seeking to achieve even the existing concept of citizenship education, whether by hortatory or indoctrinating approach, by case-study approaches,[12] by discourse in a free market of ideas, by modelling democratic processes through role-playing,[13] or by a Socratic approach,[14] or by some combination of all these along a continuum from more teacher-directed to more child-centred. All will also be mightily expressive of underlying social assumptions and cultural values.[15]

But the process which is required to blend the different approaches into a personal, collegial or institutional style is far from straightforward. Rather it is subtle, professionally and personally demanding and ever-changing. It requires a personal and professional commitment and capacity for arbitration within oneself and with one's colleagues, students and the community. The results of that blending process will generate a range of teaching approaches, including some in which the educator can adopt the role of neutral facilitator. But that cannot always be the case. For presumably, if a democratic society believes in democratic values, it must equally consider them to be worth perpetuating. A democratic society was never defined as an 'anything-goes' society[16] and one of its quite legitimate and supreme purposes must be the survival of democracy, freedom and justice. Thus it should not be assumed that hortatory or heavily didactic methods within an overall approach are necessarily undemocratic and inimical to critical thinking, provided that is not the totality of approach. On the other hand the pendulum of passivity has hung so heavily over the totality of the professional practice of much that has passed for citizenship education in the past, that the time has come for change.[17]

TOWARDS AN INTERNATIONAL POLICY FOR GLOBAL CITIZENSHIP EDUCATION

The seedbed within which an effective approach to citizenship education can grow can only be the system of which it is a part. There is certainly scope for statements at international and national levels by ministries of education and analogous organizations, by professional associations of educators, by subject associations, parents and teachers groups and other community organizations. The important thing is that the market-place of ideas is free and yet regulated and that the very process of arriving at a tentative and provisional definition is itself recognized as an educational experience for all parties.[18] That apparent contradiction of free but regulated process merits a further comment. The discourse should be free insofar as no one organization, individual or body has the monopoly right to define global citizenship education for all time and places. It should be regulated, insofar as it takes its imperative from human rights, justice and responsibility and recognizes the essential reciprocity of those rights, justice and responsibilities and their foundation in mutual respect for persons.

At the international level, there is still much that remains to be done, even though much progress was made during the 1980s and by the end of that decade over 50 per cent of the world's countries defined themselves as liberal democracies. In that decade too, new ground was broken in defining and codifying the international rights of children. But much still remains to be done by international and bilateral agencies to embody the principles of human rights and justice in the relationships between nations and to persuade other nations to adopt an education, expressive of those principles of human rights. It is still the case that in many countries, even signatories to international conventions and instruments apparently securing human rights, the rights of women, children, religious and ethnic minorities, migrant workers and others are still openly and covertly flouted. Many nations, not least in the Middle East, are still educating for hate and violence, for religious superiority and for national glory and conquest. What appears to be needed is an international conference on human rights and education, a kind of Jomtien II, to focus international attention on the important function of human rights in education at all levels, leading to the kind of action papers and agreements, including regional and international monitoring of compliance, which resulted from the International Conference on Education for All.

Such a conference could take as its guiding principles some of the principles to be found in various United Nations human rights instruments and declarations:

(a) acceptance into their own law of the principles of the United Nations Charter and the International Declarations on Human Rights, including agreements on the rights of women, children, the disabled, migrant workers and their families;

(b) agreement on the part of all countries to allow their citizens recourse to international courts for redress of the infringement of individual citizen's rights by the state;

(c) acceptance of the rights of all world citizens to freedom of religious activity in any country, to freedom of movement regardless of sex and to gender equity;

(d) recognition of cultural diversity as a characteristic of democratic society and of the contemporary world;

(e) recognition of human rights and the rule of their law as the basic principles and ethic of each nation's education system and an undertaking not to use the education systems for the purposes of the excitement of national, ethnic, religious or cultural hatred;

(f) commitment by each nation to educate its citizens for ethnic, national and international citizenship, reciprocal responsibilities and global solidarity;

(g) acceptance of world economic and environmental interdependence and the need to review that interdependence against principles of universal human justice;

(h) commitment to a concept of knowledge and its dissemination which is equitable, world-open in the sense that it reflects the experience of different groups, communities, nations and regions, the experience of men and women and of different religious, ethnic and racial traditions;

(i)   acceptance of the need for education in creative conflict resolution at personal, intergroup, national and international levels and to enable learners, through encounter with controversial issues, to base judgements on reasonable evidence and not on bias and emotion.

These principles would then be incorporated into the ethic of each nation's educational system and become the mainspring for its development. Together with human rights, they would provide the overarching value system, part of the knowledge systems and the determinants of structures, processes and procedures, professional conduct and service, afforded by those systems. Of course, there are major difficulties in developing an international human rights and values led education, where one did not exist before. As Tarrow had indicated, such problems include such matters as the imprecise definition of citizenship education, uncertainty about its prospective place in the curriculum, dissonance between its aims and content and its strategies, the poverty and paucity of existing materials, the lack of professional social systems to sustain it, poor or non-existent evaluation, inadequate systemic support for teachers, lack of professional preparation on the part of educators, and finally and very tellingly, the perception of a clash between education and global citizenship.[19]

On the other hand, the very process of defining and dialoging about basic principles for a global human rights education is the beginning of the process of overcoming these difficulties. That the field is young and ill-defined and resourced is beyond doubt. So let us share a definition of human rights education which could provide the mainspring for the kind of global citizenship education advocated in this book:

> Human rights education is the basic moral education of all students. It provides the values for the content, structure and process of all education at all levels and in all modes. It is, at the same time, part of the content of education and the provider of the criteria by which decisions about education are validated and legitimated. It, thus provides ethical guidelines for the organization of education, internationally, nationally, institutionally and instructionally in all dimensions: aims and intentions, content, procedures and processes, assessment and evaluation.[20]

Certainly, there will need to be more advocacy of a global approach to citizenship education before it will be accepted, even by those nations which are currently teaching education for citizenship. Yet there is evidence that in such nations as the United States, Canada, Australia and the United Kingdom, there is a move towards placing citizenship education within a global context. What is required now is for the educators to pick up the relay of the principles and definition indicated above and to incorporate them into the systemic aims for education in culturally diverse societies (see Chapter 2, p. 36).

As at the national level, such aims for education in culturally diverse societies can be focused more sharply on the task of education for 'global citizenship transmission'. Their purpose would be to provide the seedbed of appropriate international values, from which can grow subsequent decisions and judgements about the values and knowledge, concepts and skills, which should be transmitted, about the procedures for their transmission, about desirable behaviour in differing social contexts, times and places, about what should be rewarded and punished and what is the best form of social participation, about what citizenship means and should mean in different spheres of activity, such as political, economic (both as consumer and worker), cultural, environmental, etc.

Certainly, to use such a technique is not unprecedented. It is the use of an ideal concept of citizen and an ideal concept of society, although this time it is a global concept of citizen and a global concept of human society. But, since time immemorial, humankind has generated ideals for higher levels of moral behaviour and human creativity. Professionals and others continue to use the technique in the democratic advancement of their case.[21] This process is, in essence, no different except that it seeks to build on over two thousand years of striving for a better 'good', defined within national parameters, and to substitute a definition appropriate to the twentieth century.

Of course, I accept that many of the policy statements in contiguous areas of educational endeavour, such as multicultural education, law-related education and gender equity have not been very successful. But then, no one has ever argued that they are sufficient alone. Indeed the reverse is the case, namely that they are a necessary but not sufficient basis for the development, in this case, of a policy of global citizenship education. Additionally, there is another problem, which was, for example, encountered in the teaching of Canada's human rights charter after the patriation of the Canadian Constitution, namely that until such instruments have been interpreted at a higher level, including a higher legal level in the courts, it is very difficult for authoritative and definitive interpretations to be incorporated into textbooks and curricula.[22]

It could, however, be argued that both the Canadian Charter and such United States legislation and judgements as the Brown decision of 1954 (declaring racial segregation illegal) and the Public Law 94–142 of 1975 (concerning the education of handicapped children) have been influential, not only in North America, but beyond its geographical borders as well, in so far as they set a context for a growing ideology of greater racial and handicap justice in other countries worldwide. Moreover, as in the case of the Bill of Rights in the United States, the instrument may provide not only values for institutional integration, but also models for teaching approaches at the instructional levels.[23] Then too a nation's abuse of the human rights of its citizens may retrospectively provide grist to the mill of a strengthening of those rights, their incorporation into systemic and institutional policy and instructional material and methods.[24] On the other hand, it is evident that a systemic framework is no more than that. In addition to that systemic framework and ideology, the values of global citizenship education must be internalized into the professional consciousness and practice of each school, each student and each teacher.

TOWARDS AN INSTITUTIONAL POLICY FOR GLOBAL CITIZENSHIP EDUCATION

Just as an institutional policy for global citizenship education requires a systemic basis, so does an instructional one require an institutional basis. The school has to seek to provide the ethos and structures, processes and procedures, activities and knowledge opportunities to implement the above principles. Again, the school's provision is a framework for learning. It is important, but insufficient by itself. It needs the support and interaction of the systemic and instructional levels. On the other hand, its reach to the point of learning is closer than the systemic level, and it can have a more direct impact and a more flexible and iterative relationship with its learning clients. In Chapter 2 (pp. 40–41) I gave a list of principles to which it should adhere. To summarize briefly, these should include:

(a) an ordered environment
(b) a respect and concern for others
(c) achievement of full intellectual emotional, physical, spiritual and moral potential
(d) an appreciation of human achievements in all fields
(e) an ethos of mutuality and reciprocity
(f) the development of self-esteem, self-confidence and social responsibility
(g) a concept of 'environmental stewardship'
(h) economic literacy
(i) preparation for active local, national and global citizenship.

Within the context of such principles, each school will need to develop a policy on education for global citizenship as part of the overall goals of the school. The statement of the policy must have a mechanism for continual review and evaluation through a process of participatory democracy, and it will deal with all aspects of school life, including external relations. The statement will encapsulate an overall institutional philosophy and make explicit reference to negotiated rules, which enable the institution to function in an orderly, humane and just manner. Within that will be the philosophy of teaching and learning for global citizenship.

TOWARDS AN INSTRUCTIONAL POLICY FOR GLOBAL CITIZENSHIP EDUCATION

An instructional commitment to human rights and global citizenship education is concerned with more than the teaching and learning strategies adopted by the teacher, although those strategies represent the essential core of effective global citizenship education. What I have referred to as the instructional level, is really concerned with the overall context of interactions which the school can influence either directly through regulation or indirectly through the ethos, which it 'broadcasts' to its staff, students, parents and community. It is concerned with the whole spectrum of interaction between pupils and pupils, pupils and teachers, teachers and teachers, teachers and parents and the school and the wider community, through both formal and non-formal channels. For much of this interaction, perhaps the bulk of the students' time in education, the teacher will not be present, indeed no formal representative of the authority of the school will be present, whether in the recreational breaks, in the informal life of the school corridors and entrances, in the school bus or in interactions well beyond the jurisdiction of the school and the teachers. It is not least from that whole spectrum that the baseline values and attitudes for learning will be set for both parties in the narrower instructional process. Elsewhere, I suggested nine basic principles as a basis for professional decisions and the selection of appropriate teaching and learning strategies:

(a)   respect for persons, including all members of the school community;
(b)   open, democratic, accepting and participatory classroom climate;
(c)   active commitment to global human rights in all teaching and learning;
(d)   incorporation of the democratic process into instructional process;
(e)   provision of a supportive environment which encourages creative and reflective thinking and personal values clarification;
(f)   encouragement of moral engagement for human rights, dignity and justice;
(g)   development of higher-level thinking;
(h)   fostering of communicative competence across cultures;
(i)   encouragement of engagement with both means and ends, including those of global citizenship education.[25]

There are five major elements within the construction of an instructional policy: *ethical and moral education*, including such issues as unethical economic behaviour by individuals and nations;[26] *critical and reflexive thinking*; *knowledge of and expertise in the democratic process* (this includes such elements as cooperative modes of working); *a developmental approach to the evolution of global citizenship education*, attentive to the growth of the child; and *active commitment to human rights and social responsibilities* at all stages and in all processes. These five elements clearly overlap and interact, but in their synergy they represent essential dimensions of a philosophy of teaching and learning for global citizenship education. It follows that the effective delivery of global citizenship education within individual classrooms is as much a matter of the classroom atmosphere as it is of the method of teaching. It is as much focused on the responsiveness of the teacher, of his or her lack of bias, his or her sensitivity to human rights and orientation to children, of his or her openness to discourse as it is a matter of the children's scores.

With regard to the *moral and ethical dimension* of global citizenship education, it is important to note that there has been a gradual evolution in both the content and the approach to moral and ethical education as part of citizenship. An era in which the focus was on moral and ethical content, delivered through didactic and hortatory methods, soon after the end of the Second World War, was followed by a period of attempted value-neutrality, where the teacher was more conscious of group dynamics and pressures, in the 1960s and early 1970s. This, in turn, has been succeeded by the more recent attempts to develop the reflective and morally autonomous person as being essential to a democratic society.[27] Some now argue that the prior two stages, which one might characterize as the interventionist and the passive, were necessary early stages and pedagogical precursors of the current reflective-thinker approach. Some have argued that imaginative philosophical dialogue is an essential condition to any education,[28] but they sometimes underplay the active outcomes of such a process.

For any effective global citizenship education, the ethical base is very closely related to the ability to make practical judgements and rational decisions, using human rights as the yardstick. This connection between moral and ethical principles, the development of higher-order thinking and practical decision-making and behaviour, what might be called practical ethical reasoning,[29] applies across all the levels of citizenship introduced in the first chapter as well as in all the domains: cultural, social, political, economic and environmental. It is not necessary to be a moral developmentalist, and to believe that the moral development of children progresses irreversibly through a series of predefined moral stages, to realize that it is also interdependent with the level and age of the students.[30] Unethical economic behaviour on the part of individuals, groups and societies, for example, is deeply rooted in the political and social context of the institutions and societies within which individuals are educated,[31] and schools need to combat such economic prejudice as much as the often more manifest credal, ethnic, gender or racial kind. More, schools must demonstrate democratic human-rights-based values in their structure and personnel policies as much as in their personal relations and curricula.[32]

It is an apparent paradox to demand that schools provide moral education at a time when pluralist societies appear to be so confused about the values which they espouse. None the less, because it is such a crucial agency of socialization, a school must make explicit and available for challenge by any of its members, the moral principles and social values by which it wishes to judge and be judged and the methods by which it intends to achieve its 'moral' goals.[33] This will entail a balance between intellectual and experiential approaches, between classroom and community learning, between academic and interpersonal learning and between theoretical judgement and practical action. This book argues that human rights, in any case, provide the shared basis for such an educational enterprise. All schools must support peaceful conflict resolution, at interpersonal, intergroup and international levels, both in theory and in practice.

It is interesting to note that historically, in the United States at least, the development of reasoning ability, including decision-making competences, was deeply embedded in the early assumptions about socializing newly arriving immigrants into a complex social, economic and political fabric. For all its passivity and lack of sophistication, such an approach recognized that the second element, *critical and reflexive thinking*, is closely related to the previous element of ethical and moral development. While some writers have traced the newer imperative for critical thinking somewhat mechanically and uncritically back to the work of John Dewey[34] and have not allowed for newer orientations, it is clear that the novel reflective inquiry approaches of the 1980s represented a change in quality if not in principle, with their emphasis on the acquisition of the modes of scientific inquiry and the knowledge-gathering skills of the social scientist.[35]

Clearly, a broad range of ethical and moral considerations are located within any decision-making model, for these elements provide the criteria against which such decisions can be made and problems or issues resolved. Some writers have argued that, alone, skill in rational decision-making is significantly related to political participation.[37] But, inherent in the classic decision-making model derived from psychology are problems about the natural limitations of human rationality and thinking and at least four key elements to the rational decision-making process: the problem or issue to be decided; the alternative courses of action; the consequences; and the values.[37]

With regard to classroom practice for rational decision-making, it is evident that mere exhortation is unlikely to produce the desired effects. Other classroom and institutional processes are needed, and these were the focus of the 'new social studies' in the early 1980s.[38] Students need to become competent in the formulation and testing of hypotheses and the more general application of the techniques of scientific inquiry to issues, topics and problems, in order to develop decision-making competence. The school must recognize that reflective inquiry as a method for the acquisition of thinking skills implies the acceptance of the provisionality of human meaning and the continuous participation by learners in the process of meaning reconstruction. Equally, as Dewey described, individuals interact with their social environment, that is the school in our case, in testing and evaluating their interpretation of reality and for evaluating their judgements and decisions. For that reason alone, great care needs to be taken in the construction of the instructional (and institutional) environment.

Much has been written concerning *knowledge of and expertise in the democratic process*, including such elements as cooperative modes of working. Education for global citizenship, as defined in this book, is an experiential and liberating preparation for incumbency of a multilevel citizenship, committed to human rights and deriving an ethical or moral core from those human rights. That process, addressing cognitive, affective and conative goals for the reconstruction of social relations at local, national and international levels, has to be commenced in the school, and more especially within the instructional relationship. In that task, the educator may well return to the work of Dewey, with its emphasis on problem-solving, political decision-making and discovery by the child through interaction with the social and physical environment and the development of understanding and empathy.[39] The teacher has to develop the instructional context within which the child can construct his or her own reflective and humane system of values within the context of a democratic institution and classroom environment, which is expressive of a democratic society. Such a goal inevitably requires a reflective inquiry approach to learning and to professional practice and self-appraisal, in which the bounds of the exploration are not preset, but are themselves open to critical appraisal.

The momentum of a democratic classroom approach is generated by attentiveness in teaching and learning to human rights, justice and responsibilities, so that the reality of the classroom and school are jointly and dialogically reconstructed into the democratic reality of the wider community, society and the global context within which we all live. Thus creative participation in the teaching/learning process and reflection of the rights and duties of citizens in free societies towards each other and to those less fortunate are indispensable elements in this process. An appropriate classroom strategy for global citizenship education implies the prior construction of a microcosm of the just world society. The two-way interdependence of the levels of citizenship is underlined, for a non-democratic institution cannot really prepare for democracy, any more than a non-just society can really deliver justice.

With regard to *developmental stages*, it is important to note the early stage of human development at which prejudice, ethnic bigotry and gender bias may be learned as part of a stereotyping process, based on false generalization. Equally, citizenship concepts such as justice or fair play begin to develop early in children and can thus be fostered through the right kind of activity as part of an ongoing and coherent experience throughout the school life of the child.[40,41] Educators must develop children's skills of dialectical thinking, through such strategies as values clarification, principle-testing, statistical analysis, valid categorization and generalization, analysis of cause-and-effect relationships, distinguishing between relevant and irrelevant information, arguments and principles, clarification and exposure of unstated assumptions, inferential recognitions and dissection of different points of view.[42]

Recent work by Dynneson and Gross has attempted to construct a six-part theoretical model for citizenship education, matched to the developmental levels of children and their social development.[43] The first stage is that of what is termed *biological citizenship*, where the child is almost totally dependent for its social relationships as for all else on its mother. This is an important stage for the beginnings of generalizations and attributions, as in the case of colour. The second stage is that of *family citizenship*, where the child's social world expands to include a wider circle of family and friends and some of its assumptions are challenged, others reinforced. The third stage is that of *nonbiological social relationships*, where the child comes into contact with peers outside the family, and ultimately in the school. Here the first scientific approaches to categorization and generalization occur for most children, through such work as setting in mathematics and the placing of human beings and groups, their culture and behaviour and physical objects in similar or identical sets. Reception-class teachers have the opportunity and power to work mightily for cooperative citizenship and against prejudice and stereotypical representation.

Next comes the stage of *stratified social citizenship*, where the development of social categorization is strengthened and membership behaviour grows. This is clearly a crucial stage for the development of concepts of cooperative citizenship as also for the development or eradication of prejudiced or stereotypical views of other people, their cultural values and mores, their appearance, their race, ethnicity and nationality. Stage five is the period of *horizontally expanded citizenship*, where peer-group relationships exert extraordinarily strong influence. Occurring predominantly in early adolescence, this is a crucial time for the development of autonomous, but socially responsible, citizenship. Finally, there is the stage of *vertically expanded citizenship*, where new group social relationships are developed, and the search commences for stability between and within groups; a time of search for social order and structure among groups. These six stages all have their own demands in terms of educational strategies, which educators need to take into account in the design and delivery of citizenship education.

Turning now to the fifth element, the development of an *active commitment to human rights and social responsibilities*, we find that the field is young, ill-defined and poorly resourced at all levels, although new instructional materials are now beginning to emerge. Yet, human rights education which can provide the mainspring for the kind of global citizenship education that forms part of the basic moral education of all students for the whole of their lives, in school and out, during school and in their adult years. It not only provides the values for the content, structure and process of all education at all levels and in all modes, but is also, at the same time, part of the content of education and the provider of the criteria by which decisions about education are validated. Human rights education thus provides ethical guidelines for the organization of education, internationally, nationally, institutionally and instructionally in all dimensions: aims and intentions, content, procedures and processes, assessment and evaluation.[44]

Further, at the base of global citizenship education, committed to human rights, justice and social responsibility, is the so-called 'rule of law'. In educating for social responsibilities, we need an instructional relationship which encourages the assumption of duties, responsibilities and obligations by young people. For just as the very foundation of a free society is law, so also the preparation for that society in school has to take place where decisions and judgement, relationships and learning are neither capricious nor arbitrary, but are law-guided, for without such laws and school regulations, no one is free. So there is a system of checks and balances, with many of the competencies to be developed being the same as those which address the other side of the coin of citizenship education: human rights. A system of mediation and arbitration, in which individuals can be critically but constructively responsive to legitimate authority and know what rights are and how they can best be secured, is essential; this has deep implications for the design of classroom practice.[45]

This classroom practice must involve the development of the ability of both teacher and taught to negotiate and to achieve creative compromise in cultural, social, economic and environmental spheres, rather than to 'imbibe' inert preordained knowledge and values.[46] It implies participation in social change at school and community levels, in order to engage for the values and ideals of human rights and freedoms. To relate back to the second of the major elements listed above, skills of critical thinking and problem-solving must interact with personal and intergroup social skills essential to pluralist democracy and the creative management of change. Classroom practice will be influenced by what has been called resistance pedagogy, which encourages the learner to critique the immediate society of the school and classroom against its own declared values (and one might add the values of international human rights). It stimulates the learner to imagine alternative teaching or learning relationships, and encourages the exploration of dilemmas and contradictions. Paulo Freire has described this, as I have argued earlier, as a process of identification.[47]

The impact is inevitably to set up pressures not only for the just society but also for the just school society, with checks and balances to safeguard the rights and freedoms of individuals and to apportion public and private responsibility. There will also be recognition of the need for such activities as participation, social service, community self-help and philanthropy to be encouraged as desirable civic values. Such basic values must permeate any teaching/learning approaches in classrooms and schools within democratic, pluralist societies. Indeed, it is only through education that they may be perpetuated.

As pointed out in the last chapter, however, it is important to note that such values are often contested territory, and that even where that is not the case, it is accepted that both students and teachers need to derive and clarify reflectively their own coherent set of values, and in the case of teachers the rationale for teaching which derives from those values. This is particularly the case for those teachers who carry a special responsibility for citizenship education in the sense in which it is being used in this book, as process equally as much as product. For active citizenship something more than hand-me-down information and attitudes towards citizenship is required. Students need to develop skills in obtaining information, judging its value and reaching sound conclusions, based on evidence. They need to acquire information through different media and senses, to select and organize it, and to express it clearly in speech and writing. But they need more. What is needed in addition is an attitude to citizenship which enables the individual to make moral and humane judgements and take actions on the basis of values of their own, which are congruent with the values, rights and freedoms cited above. With such an attitude students can become effective civic actors and decision-makers, able to cope with and creatively live with the conflicts inherent within all pluralist societies and to engage actively for human justice, rights and freedoms for all.

Clearly, there is a close interlinkage between the two elements of human rights and democratic process. For concern for human rights and social responsibilities is 'a way of life' and at its core is the ethic of respect for all persons: the realization that human rights are indivisible. As I argued in the last chapter, those human rights transcend the social domain and reach into economic and environmental domains. However imperfectly, such an ethic and such rights are embedded within democratic societies and are locked in place by the laws of that society. This is one of the major differences between democratic and non-democratic societies. But, while the aims and ethic may be confined to democratic societies in their practice at the moment, their implications and application transcend those societies and are in that respect global.

These five elements together form the guidelines for the ways in which the teacher may structure the learning environment, and an iterative basis for the teacher's own learning and teaching goals. The principles underlying an instructional policy might include:

(a) commitment to a democratic ethos within school and classroom as the basis for enhancing both cognitive and social learning;

(b) shared decision-making, with appeal to the judgement of students, including decisions on learning objectives and content;

(c) acceptance of the importance of varied and cooperative modes of learning, and the legitimacy of different paces and styles of learning;

(d) commitment to accountability and due process in all professional judgements;

(e) fostering of the skills of advocacy, arbitration, mediation and discourse to resolve conflicts between teachers and pupils and among teachers and pupils;

(f) acceptance of the confidentiality of pupil's personal lives and records, insofar as they wish it;

(g) acceptance of the right of students to see their own school records:

(h) acceptance of the affective dimension in controversial issues and the resolution of moral dilemmas;

(i) acceptance of the provisionality and tentativeness of human knowledge and professional judgements;

(j) development of joint modes of assessment and evaluation;

(k) fostering of interpersonal relations within an overall commitment to respect for persons;

(l) provision of a coherent focus on human rights and social responsibilities at local, national and international levels and across social, economic, environmental and political domains.

In this chapter, I have argued that global citizenship education demands a whole school approach and commitment, integrated and sequentially expressed and cooperatively planned and implemented, backed up by specific location within the curriculum and enforced through criteria and formative principles of procedure, subject to regular review. To commence that process of review and in concert with the principles of procedure, which have been used throughout this volume, we now need to subject the ideas and proposals introduced in this chapter to a reflexive reappraisal and personal and institutional scrutiny.

PROFESSIONAL VALIDATION

Clearly the above principles, which might underlie policy for the delivery of global citizenship education, also form the basis for the development of both institutional and individual philosophies of teaching. In the spirit of the principle of provisionality, however, it is important to ask to what extent they are viable for each school and each individual. This will inevitably include a review of what already exists and is being done and a consideration of the existing school ethos. The questions to be asked might include:

(a)   Are the different levels of commitment suggested in this chapter expressed in your school?

(b)   Is there a mission statement for the school which identifies the basic principles on which it works?

(c)   Do your procedures for review and evaluation include attentiveness to human rights and global social responsibilities?

(d)   Is citizenship education already taught and how?

(e)   How far do colleagues make explicit their philosophy of teaching and how far does it coincide with the twelve principles outlined above?

(f)   How can you interest colleagues in the further development of a global citizenship dimension to the curriculum and the adoption of a human-rights-driven provision of schooling?

(g)   How far do methods of assessment and control in the school adopt basic legal processes, attentive to individual human rights?

(h)   In what ways is the teaching of citizenship developmentally sensitive to the growth of the child?

Building on the answers to such questions, in the next chapter we shall be looking in greater detail at the instructional options available for the delivery of global citizenship education.

NOTES AND REFERENCES

1.   Carter, T. L. (1988) 'Application of organization development theory and practice to improve citizenship'. Dissertation presented for the degree of Doctor of Education at the University of Seattle.

2.   Rutter, R. A. (1985) 'Political socialization in high school: a study of contradictory school messages, student mediation and political attitudes', unpublished PhD dissertation, University of Wisconsin–Madison.

3.   Radz, M. A. (1988) 'The school building: key to citizenship education', *Social Studies Supervisors Association Newsletter*, **3**(2), 8–9.

4.   The programme sought to promote civic participation, democratic values and also academic and critical thinking skills. See Pereira, C. (1988) 'Educating for citizenship in the elementary grades', *Phi Delta Kappan*, **69**(6), 429–31.

5.   Parker, W. C. (1988) 'Why ethics in citizenship education?', *Social Studies and the Young Learner*, **1**(1), 3–5.

6.   See, for example, The National Curriculum Council (1990) *Education for Citizenship* (York: National Curriculum Council); Remy, R. C. (1980) *Citizenship and Consumer Education: Key Assumptions and Basic Competencies* (Bloomington, IN: Phi Delta Kappa Educational

Foundation); Barth, J. L. (1988) 'A consistent social studies definition, rationale and goals for developing responsible citizenship', *Social Studies Teacher*, 9(2), 198ff; and Wooster, J. S. (1985) 'Citizenship education in the K-6 New York State Social Studies Program', *Social Science Record*, 22(1), 26-7.

7. One author argues that such variability means that citizenship education has such long-term objectives as to make it difficult, if not impossible, for teachers to deliver it. See Sutherland, M. B. (1981) 'The impossibilities of education for citizenship' (The 1981 Sera Lecture), *Scottish Educational Review*, 13(1), 5-11.

8. Chesteen, R. D. (1980) 'A report on national programs in citizenship and law-related education', Martin: University of Tennessee.

9. Giroux, H. A. (1987) 'Citizenship, public philosophy and the struggle for democracy', *Educational Theory*, 37(2), 103-20.

10. Torney-Purta, J. and Schwille, J. (1982) 'The values learned in school: policy and practice in industrialized countries', paper presented at a meeting of the National Commission on Excellence in Education. Washington, DC: National Commission on Excellence in Education.

11. See, for example, Drake, C. (1987) 'Educating for responsible global citizenship', *Journal of Geography*, 86(6), 300-6.

12. Snell, D. (1989) 'Classroom case studies', *History and Social Science Teacher*, 24(2), 90-2.

13. Hickey, M. G. (1990) 'Mock trials for children', *Social Education*, 54(1), 43-4; and Popenfus, J. R. and Kimbrell, M. (1989) 'The mock trial as an activity in high school', *History and Social Science Teacher*, 25(1), 35-7.

14. Ealy, D. S. (1990) 'Talking in the marketplace: a new approach to political philosophy', *Political Science Teacher*, 3(1), 15, proposes the utilization of a model of Socratic discussion in teaching politics.

15. Shaver, J. P. (1986) 'Reflections on citizenship education and traditional social studies programs', *Georgia Social Science Journal*, 17(3), 1-15.

16. This issue is discussed in Shaver, J. P. (1985) 'Commitment to values and the study of social problems in citizenship education', *Social Education*, 49(3), 194-7.

17. Shermis, S. S. and Barth, J. L. (1982) 'Teaching for passive citizenship: a critique of philosophical assumptions', *Theory and Research in Social Education*, 10(4), 17-37.

18. Gutmann, A. (1987) *Democratic Education* (Princeton, NJ: Princeton University Press).

19. Tarrow, N. (1988) *Human Rights and Education* (Oxford: Pergamon Press), and (1988) 'Human rights education: a comparison of Canadian and US approaches', paper presented at the Comparative and International Education Society, Western Regional Conference, Sacramento, CA, 21 October.

20. I have utilized a similar definition in a previous publication. See Lynch, J. (1989) *Multicultural Education in a Global Society* (London: Falmer Press), p. 81.

21. See, for example, Arends, R. I. and Thomas, T. (1987) 'Getting law-related education into the curriculum so that it stays: messages from research and some guidelines for action', *International Journal of Social Education* 2(2), 19-36.

22. Snell, D. (1989) 'Teaching Canada's charter', *History and Social Science Teacher* 24(2), 71-2.

23. One example of this is Aldridge, K. and Wray, J. (1988) 'Students' constitutional rights', *Update on Law-Related Education* 12(1), 30-3.

24. Wright, I. (1987) 'Social studies and law-related education: a case study of the Japanese in British Columbia', *History and Social Science Teacher* 22(4), 209-14.

25. I have slightly amended the original list. See Lynch, J. (1989) *Multicultural Education in a Global Society* (London: Falmer Press) p. 112.

26. An interesting article in this respect is Schug, M. C. (1988) 'Economic values and values education', *Social Studies and the Young Learner*, 1(1), 6-9.

27. A brief summary of this evolution is contained in Ryan, K. (1986) 'The new moral education', *Phi Delta Kappan* 68(4), 228-33.

28. Sharp, M. A. (1986) 'Is there an essence of education?', *Journal of Moral Education* 15(3), 189-96.

29. Lockwood, A.L. (1985) 'A place for ethical reasoning in the social studies curriculum', *Social Studies* **76**(6), 264–8.
30. Malikail, J.S. and Stewart, J.D. (1987) *Personal and Social Values and Skills: A Study Completed for the Saskatchewan Department of Education Core Curriculum Investigation Project* (Regina, Saskatchewan: Regina University Faculty of Education).
31. Schug, M.C. (1988) 'Economic reasoning and values education', *Social Studies and the Young Learner*, **1**(1), 6–9.
32. See Gluckman, I.B. (1984) 'Values education in the public schools', *NASSP Bulletin*, **68**(470), 98–104.
33. Wicks, R.S. (1981) *Morality and the Schools* (Washington, DC: Council for Basic Education).
34. Dewey, J. (1910) *How We Think* (Boston: D.C. Heath).
35. Barr, R.D., Barth, J.L. and Shermis, S.S. (1977) *Defining the Social Studies* (Arlington, VA: National Council for the Social Studies).
36. See the paper by Guyton, E.A. (1982) 'Critical thinking and political participation: the development and assessment of a causal model', paper presented at the Annual Meeting of the National Council for the Social Studies, Boston, MA, 23–7 November.
37. Milburn, T.W. and Billings, R.S. (1976) 'Decision-making perspectives from psychology', *American Behavioral Scientist*, **20**(1), 111–26.
38. Massialas, B.G. and Hurst, J.B. (1978) *Social Studies in a New Era: The School as a Laboratory for Real Life Experiences* (New York: Longman).
39. Dewey, J. (1916) *Democracy and Education* (New York: Macmillan).
40. Wright, I. (1988) 'Citizenship education and decision-making', *International Journal of Social Education*, **3**(2), 55–62.
41. For example, Kneedler, P.E. (1988) 'Assessment of critical thinking skills in History/Social Science', *Social Studies Review*, **27**(3), 2–93.
42. An interesting article from which some of these examples were taken is Rudin, B. (1984) 'Teaching critical thinking skills', *Social Education*, **48**(4), 279–81.
43. Dynneson, T.L. and Gross, R.E. (1985) 'An eclectic approach to citizenship: developmental stages', *The Social Studies*, **76**(1), 23–7.
44. I have utilized a similar definition in a previous publication. See Lynch, J. (1989) *Multicultural Education in a Global Society* (London: Falmer Press), p. 81.
45. Anderson, C.C. (1980) 'Promoting responsible citizenship through elementary law-related education', *Social Education*, **44**(5), 383–6.
46. For more details of the kind of specific skills needed for creative citizenship, see Remy, R.C. (1980) *Handbook of Basic Citizenship Competencies* (Alexandria, VA: Association for Supervision and Curriculum Development).
47. Freire, P. (1973) *Education for Critical Consciousness* (New York: Seabury Press).

Chapter 4

School and Classroom Practice

INTRODUCTION

Drawing upon the conceptualization introduced at the end of Chapter 2, the third chapter proposed goals related to the structure, processes and content of global citizenship education at the international, systemic and instructional levels. The main aim of this chapter is to translate the macro and micro policy and process considerations and criteria proposed in Chapter 3 to the micro level of the school, the classroom and the curriculum. In that task, our concern is two-fold, firstly, the content of the planned curriculum and secondly, the process by which the planned curriculum for global citizenship education may best be delivered in school and classroom. By curriculum, I mean all of the activities and learning planned by the school and not solely the syllabus. Both school and classroom will contribute to both of these areas. This does not mean that we can neglect the informal and unintended curriculum, which can exercise such a powerful influence on students' attitudes and behaviour, or the unintended consequences of the planned curriculum or the effects of the hidden curricula of home, community, mass media and society in general. Rather any planned curriculum needs to be able to take these influences into account.

For purposes of analysis only, the chapter is divided into two parts: school activities and classroom activities. It is focused on the planned curriculum in school and classroom. A set of basic values for global citizenship education, as proposed in the work of R. Freeman Butts, is suggested as a working basis for a tentative plan for school and classroom practice. A rationale for the content of citizenship education is developed, drawing on the principles of procedure adopted throughout this book. Examples of both school and classroom practice are given, and model teaching approaches are identified from practice in a number of different countries.

At the instructional level, the five elements of global citizenship education outlined in the last chapter (the ethical and moral orientation of citizenship education; critical and reflexive thinking; knowledge of and expertise in the democratic process; a developmental approach, attentive to the growth of the child; an active commitment to human rights and social responsibilities) are illustrated from a more practical point of view. An attempt is made to link the proposals contained in this chapter with the research on effective schools and classrooms and on productive teaching and learning.

There will be descriptions derived from the work of the Council of Europe and analogous developments in Australia, Canada, the United States and other countries. This chapter tries to provide for each teacher an individual plan from a synthesis of teaching/learning strategies, which individual teachers may absorb into their own professional style of teaching in pursuit of global citizenship education. A continuum of different approaches along the range from direct to vicarious methods is introduced and commented on, founded on both intellectual and experiential teaching/learning strategies; and at the institutional level a range of strategies, such as twinning, intervisiting and interlinking, as well as activity methods such as role-playing and simulation, audio-visual and computer approaches, is suggested. Finally, and once again, there is a professional dialogue with the readers to encourage them to take critical distance from the proposals being made and to measure them against their own professional judgement, context and personal teaching style.

VALUES FOR SCHOOL AND CLASSROOM PRACTICE

In some subject areas, both values and principles of procedure would appear to follow with a compelling logic from the working methods and substance of the home-base discipline. This is, by and large, the case with such subjects as religious education, history, philosophy and moral education. Thus there is in a sense a ready-made set of principles for classroom practice. In the case of citizenship education, however, the home-base discipline of political science has until recently been relatively silent on classroom and school practice,[1] and the field has been left to such disciplines as social studies, history, geography and to interdisciplinary approaches from the new area of curriculum studies. That situation is both advantageous and disadvantageous to the task of defining principles for school and classroom practice. On the one hand, it forces us to make explicit a set of such principles drawn from outside the discipline and to expose some otherwise taken-for-granted assumptions. On the other hand, because the home-base discipline is concerned more with the discipline as scientific inquiry than with the normative apparatus which underlies its implementation, we are compelled to seek value bases for action elsewhere than in the home-base discipline itself. This split creates a danger of dislocation between the intellectual and academic progress of the discipline and its implementation in schools and classrooms.

In an influential publication, Butts has advocated ten civic values as the core of citizenship education in the United States: justice, freedom, equality, diversity, authority, privacy, due process, participation, personal obligation for the public good, and international human rights.[2] These core values represent an attempt to do precisely what the aim of this volume is, namely to identify a balance of rights and responsibilities which can deliver a democratic approach to education for citizenship at community, national and international levels within a context of cultural diversity. There are interesting commonalities between the Butts so-called 'decalogue' and various human rights instruments, declarations of civic liberties and charters of rights and freedoms, such as the

Canadian Constitution and the European Charter, in that they all focus on the basic idea of human fairness and equity. They are all suitable for incorporation into a mission statement for a school or other educational institution, and into its instructional and learning philosophies.

This chapter seeks to reformulate and extend those core values into two basic areas: whole-school approaches and instructional strategies. In both cases, we are concerned with the way in which such values may be incorporated into the ethos, structure, processes and review procedures of the school, and thus as much with the demonstration of such values as with their expression by means of statements. As has been observed in a recent piece of research, there are some unintended limitations in the conceptualization of Butts decalogue, and to its practical implementation. These limitations need to be taken into account when using the decalogue as guidance for the practice of global citizenship education at school and classroom levels.[3]

For example, although all the values draw on the concept of respect for persons, this is not utilized either as a category or as a master value. Equally, the implication of equality (one of the values) and respect for persons is mutuality and reciprocity, leading in turn to the ability to empathize justice (or injustice) with others and to the acceptance that what I apply to you applies to me and vice versa. Further the idea of social responsibility, which I have emphasized in each succeeding chapter of this book, is only obliquely covered by the concept of authority. Finally, as with the anthropocentric nature of much contemporary social-science theorizing, it underplays the environmental dimension, which is one of the knowledge domains of global citizenship education, as conceptualized in this book.[4]

I would suggest, therefore, that we adopt a modification of the decalogue to recognize the higher-order value of respect for persons across the domains of knowledge, with the values of justice, freedom, reciprocity (which can embrace the concepts of mutuality and equality), diversity (obviously applying at all levels of citizenship), social responsibility (which can include the concepts of duty and the legitimate use and observation of authority), privacy, due process, participation, personal obligation for the public good, commitment to the principles of international human rights, and good environmental stewardship. Using this amended version of the decalogue, I intend in this chapter to operationalize the concept of global citizenship education at the school and classroom levels.

To summarize, I am proposing that we accept that at the base of the decalogue is the fundamental idea of 'respect for persons'. This would be the master or key value. This does not mean that all behaviours and judgements are acceptable and justified. It is not a licence for 'anything goes'. The concept of respect for persons is embedded within an agreed and promulgated set of principles or values (e.g. the decalogue), which all parties agree are mutual and reciprocal in the sense of applying to all parties individually and in their relationships with each other. Respect for persons means that all members of the school community, students included, are entitled equally to all of the core values, such as justice, due process, etc. In that sense, the values are an exposition of the concept of the equally just society, identified by Rawls and introduced earlier in this book under the first priority principle of *equal basic liberties,*[5] a formulation which intertwines the ideas of freedom, justice and equality as the foundations of the equally just society.

Thus we have a hierarchy of interrelated values: the master value of respect for persons, amplified by the amended decalogue, and amplified in turn by human rights instruments and agreements. By extrapolation the concept of equal basic liberties applies, as I argued in Chapter 1, not just to the single society, but also to the global society. And if to both of those, then also to the microcosm of the school and classroom. So the foundations of a just global, national, institutional and instructional community imply the equal right of each person to the most extensive system of equal basic liberties consistent with a similar system for all as a fundamental principle. The concept of a just *institutional* and *instructional* society will need to embrace in critical questioning many of the legal, economic and social taken-for-granteds of current education and schooling in the wealthy Western democracies, on which international instruments and many national proclamations of justice maintain a relative though eloquent silence.

More specifically, and tying the concept of equal basic liberties into the previous discussion of values and institutional morality, it is evident that teachers can only fulfil their professional functions effectively if they adhere reasonably to that concept and those values. In some cases, these values may be part of the overall ideology of the teacher, influencing both the teacher's belief-system and implicit professional theories, and through them the teacher's planning, decision-making and evaluation of his or her own professional performance.[6] This aspect of value systems is particularly important to take into account for staff development purposes, and the issue of the congruence of the teacher's individual and teachers' group ideologies is an important aspect of Chapter 5 of this volume. In other cases, the values, such as intellectual integrity, may be inherent in the content or discipline.[7] Assessment, for example, demands of teacher and taught acquaintance and acceptance of the concept of due process. Allocation of resources demands application of some concept of equity. Sanctions imply the application of the concept of fairness and the acceptance of legitimate authority. In turn, the success of legitimate authority will draw on respect for the dignity of staff and students and for their legitimate right to privacy and to humanly sensitive treatment.[8]

It follows that, although we are focusing in this chapter on the school and classroom implications, equal justice cannot be limited to institutional or national frontiers; it is global. Equally, the values outlined imply that all members of the school community have the co-responsibility for achieving the social reality of those values, not only for themselves but also for others in the school and beyond. Thus the practical attainment of those values is likely to involve an exercise in the social reconstruction of the school and classroom reality.

In turn, that process implies that the school allows and empowers the challenging of ideas and behaviour which are incongruent with its stated values. The first step in that ascent is the development of a dialogue to achieve an institutional mission statement, congruent with those values; one that gives all members of the school community equal fairness in the educational enterprise. Students would, for instance, be given an automatic right to principled questioning of professional judgements about themselves, and they would be entitled to expect that assessments and curricula, school organization and procedures were culture fair and congruent with the values as codified in the institution's mission statement.

WHOLE-SCHOOL APPROACHES

No learning takes place in isolation. Rather, learning is part of an ongoing social process and context, which can facilitate or inhibit children's learning, wherever it occurs. The structure and ambience of schools, intended to facilitate children's learning, are crucial determinants of cognitive and social learning. This is more especially so where the intended learning involves values as well as cognitive increments, as is the case with global citizenship education.

In the literature, five major factors recur time and again as being correlated with effectiveness in school and instruction: strong educational leadership; high expectations of students' achievement; emphasis on basic skills; safe and orderly climate; frequent evaluation of students' progress.[9] Others which occur in some of the literature with some frequency are school ethos, achievement orientation, classroom organization and effective promulgation of school aims. Thus, there is an interactive relationship between school effectiveness factors and classroom effectiveness factors, which it is important to bear in mind in this chapter, where, for analytical purposes, I have separated practice at school and classroom levels. It is the argument of this book that the above characteristics may be used as a kind of foundation for the development of global citizenship education, either through a process of grafting additional items on top of them or by amending slightly the orientation of the original concept.

With that caveat, I turn first to the school level. In a recent publication, Stake has revisited the issue of the importance of contextual features on the success of school programmes.[10] He points to the casual and intuitive nature of our knowledge of what contextual characteristics are important. Of course, qualitative researchers have given particular attention to this aspect for some time,[11] and have attempted to define criteria for ethnographic approaches to schools, which could take this into account.[12] Then too, the effective schools movement and more recent research and writing have identified an inventory of the contextual factors which influence or determine the success of a school and can encourage the child's active participation. These factors include the principal or headteacher, the learning environment, its structure and ethos, the circumambient ethos, its vibrancy, success orientation and social and intellectual discipline. So, to sharpen the question, based on the above discussion of school strategies for global citizenship education, what educational approaches are likely to be most educationally efficient, socially productive and cost-effective? Can we weave together the above work and the wealth of material about effective schools? Is there any reason why we cannot extrapolate from the research on effective schools and teaching what is relevant for global citizenship education?

Walberg has identified those factors which are consistent, potent and generalizable, and which should be optimized, if conative, affective, and cognitive learning are to be increased: ability or prior achievement, age or stage of development, motivation and self-concept, quantity of instruction, quality of instruction, home environment, classroom environment, extra-scholastic peer-group ethos, mass media.[13] Fraser *et al.* appraised a large number of models of student learning in order to produce a model of educational productivity, including school factors, such as aims and policy, physical environment; social factors, such as socioeconomic status; instructor factors, including training and style of teaching; instructional factors, such as curriculum and quality and quantity of instruction; student factors, including gender, predisposition to learn, physical attributes; method of instruction; and learning strategy.[14] Fraser has also reviewed and summarized a large number of studies on classroom environment.[15] More recently, attempts have also been made to achieve a research synthesis of both school and instructional (classroom and environment variables) effectiveness.[16]

The effective schools movement in the United States and analogous developments elsewhere have, thus, indicated the educational inputs which are likely to be most influential in stimulating learning at school, classroom and individual levels, including the high-order importance of an ordered environment and climate for learning.[17] This aspect of an effective school, the climate or social environment, is also expressed in other publications and research. In the United Kingdom, for example, Her Majesty's Inspectorate has defined those characteristics which together are conducive to a good school, emphasizing the importance of shared values as the foundation of their corporate life.[18] Again, independent experimental research has emphasized similar factors in the identikit of an effective school, underlining the importance of the ambience or ethos of the school.[19] Ethnographic research also supports similar findings of the importance of a well-regulated environment for the construction of student–teacher relationships.[20] A rationally designed education for global citizenship can surely draw on such findings for the construction of an effective instructional and institutional strategy.

If the above argument were accepted, then, based on the existing literature,[21] a set of *organizational* and *processual* characteristics could be derived, which together would portray the school and instructional parameters within which effective global citizenship education could be delivered:

Organization

(a) strong institutional leadership committed to global citizenship education;
(b) emphasis on global citizenship education in curriculum, instruction and assessment;
(c) clear institutional and instructional goals addressing issues of citizenship;
(d) high academic, behavioural and participatory expectations for both staff and students;
(e) effective, humane and interactive evaluation and monitoring of performance;
(f) continuing professional development of staff in global citizenship education;
(g) involvement and support of parents and the community.

Process

(a) a system of strategic values and assumptions directed to human rights, social responsibility and global citizenship;
(b) a high and effective level of interaction and verbal and oral communication between all parties;
(c) collaborative planning and implementation of changes;
(d) commitment to cooperative methods in school and classrooms;

(e)   an ethos committed to human rights and democracy;
(f)   equal justice as a core value;
(g)   commitment to due process for all;
(h)   close attentiveness and congruence with children's stages of development and interests.

CLASSROOM TEACHING METHODS

The purpose of this section of the chapter is to provide examples of classroom practice which may facilitate the delivery of global citizenship education, and to interweave those examples with a spectrum of values and principles of global citizenship education across the five major elements defined in the last chapter as being indispensable to global citizenship education. Each of these elements aims to enable students gradually to develop higher levels of competence and of ability to adopt the roles and make the decisions that are required of the good citizen at the three levels outlined throughout this book.

The task of educating for global citizenship, as outlined in this book, is no easy matter, and is unlikely to be achieved by a single approach or policy. An effective global citizenship education is likely to require a combination of classroom instructional and broader whole-school enculturation strategies. But the question is quite rightly asked: are there any indispensable areas of content which have to be covered? The answer to that question is a very positive one and there have been many different attempts to summarize such content.[22] Clearly, the formulation will depend on the epistemology of the whole curriculum, including the extent to which a specific subject or curricular domain is allocated responsibility for citizenship education.

Yet, all tend to agree that there are in some form or combination the following basic areas of cognitive knowledge, which must be covered: human relations, associations and communities, seen historically and in all their contemporary diversity, including familial, local, national and international dimensions; democratic citizenship, political pluralism and pressure and interest groups, election systems, suffrage and different forms of government; communications on land, sea and in the atmosphere and beyond, through various different media; the rule of law; economic association, including responsible consumerism, wealth creation and international economic exchange; leisure and recreation; human rights and international relations and organization; human growth and development, including health, nutrition and physical and mental wellbeing; and environmental issues, including human/human, human/animal and human/biosphere issues and conservation, pollution, degradation, food and energy production, distribution and consumption. In addition, as argued in the last chapter, there are five major and indispensable dimensions or elements to global citizenship education: ethical and moral education; critical and reflexive thinking; knowledge and expertise of the democratic process; developmental approaches; and commitment to human rights and social responsibilities, with each of which we now deal in more detail.

Ethical and moral education

The Butts decalogue introduced above (see p. 66) provides a useful means of raising issues about the substantive content of moral education as a part of global citizenship education. It also provides a springboard for questions about the process by which moral values may be acquired in schools, and in what ways an educator's teaching may facilitate that process of the acquisition of the 'right' values, attuned to human rights and democratic processes. In the United States, there are basically two orientations to moral or values issues in schools. The first might be referred to as values clarification.[23] A number of models of teaching for and about values emerged in the 1960s and 1970s, many of which include moral-dilemma training, inquiry approaches and the encouragement of rational discourse.[24] More recently, Banks has proposed a value-inquiry model for values acquisition in the social studies, which encompasses nine levels: observation/discrimination; description/discrimination; identification/description; identification/analysis; hypothesizing; recalling, for example alternative values; predicting; comparing and contrasting; choosing and justifying (this latter would include stating reasons, sources and possible consequences).[25] The usefulness of the Banks model is the way that it focuses the educator's attention on the systematic way in which values acquisition has to be taught. It gives one possible schema for the rational and supportive organization of this process by educators.

The second but not entirely discrete schema is provided by the programme of justice education developed in the work of Kohlberg.[26] The moral content of Kohlberg's work is built around the liberal moral tradition of Western democratic societies and thus has a strong affinity with the moral bases of global citizenship education. But there are some weaknesses in Kohlberg's work, about which educators need to take note. For example, given that one's stage of moral development may influence one's understanding of specific moral concepts or the grounds for holding them, it does not necessarily ensure that those concepts will be acted upon. In other words, it is necessary but not sufficient. Moreover, it is important to understand that recently the work of Kohlberg has come under some criticism for its apparent ethnocentricity, gender bias and book-based approach to moral education. Notwithstanding such valid criticisms, the work of Kohlberg can still be informative at least at the theoretical level in discussing the delivery of global citizenship education. The concept of the stage typology of moral development and the basic principle that students should be taught, using material that is at a higher stage of moral development than their own, may provide basic pedagogical principles for the design of an overall strategy for the delivery of what is an intrinsically moral curriculum in global citizenship education.[27] If the only lesson from this work is that value transmission cannot be left to chance, that would be an important message. Teachers clearly cannot sit on the fence when fundamental values of human rights and democracy are at stake.

The phased introduction of materials which express moral dilemmas may enable pupils to clarify their own values and increase the moral maturity and social confidence with which they may make judgements. Where such a technique as principle-testing is used to encourage students to achieve consistency in their judgements, or to provide rational grounds for inconsistency, the basic values of global citizenship education, reciprocity, social responsibility and mutuality, may be greatly enhanced.[28] Kehoe has outlined a number of strategies which teachers may adopt to improve their effectiveness in using this technique and improving their 'aim' for the baseline values of global citizenship education.[29] In the section on developmental approaches below a phased approach is adopted to suggest content appropriate to the age and stage of the children, and this could be combined with insights from the stage typology of moral development.

There is also reciprocal value of a broader professional kind for teachers in letting the work of Kohlberg and his associates be a part of their composite teaching approach to global citizenship education, for it makes them develop good habits of listening and good question-and-answer techniques, which are sparing but revealing of the right information; they will also need to be sensitive to their own moral values and value-related decisions and judgements.[30] This work on moral reasoning reminds us that it is insufficient to simply tell pupils about moral issues or to attempt to give them a 'moral values pack' from the school store and to expect them to use it. Values development needs to be consciously planned, implemented and evaluated, but in a way which will launch the students onto moral autopilot. As a basis for such a planned approach, educators need to internalize for themselves that there is a firm foundation in human rights for objective moral good, which is formal, universal and without exception, to a greater extent than was supposed.[31]

Techniques may be used separately or combined to enable students to make decisions on rational grounds, identify alternatives, consider and take on the perspectives of others and hypothesize about consequences across time and space. Where such approaches can be combined with material and situations which are expressive of both the unity and diversity of humankind there is some evidence that students are less ethnocentric.[32] Moreover, students who frequently discuss ethical issues tend to be capable of reasoning at higher levels and may even be more capable of applying democratic principles, maintaining their own moral autonomy in the face of pressures to conform and showing concern for others.[33]

From the available evidence, it would appear that practice in rational decision-making is a major means to foster both moral development and critical and reflexive thinking. With regard to classroom practice for rational decision-making, however, mere exhortation is a weak strategy and is unlikely to produce the desired effects. Rather what is needed is a means of empowering students not only to state values and strategies, but also to demonstrate them, as evidence that both moral values and discourse expertise have been internalized.

To achieve those dual goals of values and the expertise to demonstrate them, students need to become competent in the skills of inquiry, in the formulation and testing of hypotheses and the more general application of scientific inquiry techniques to issues, topics and problems. This process implies a recognition in the school's mission that reflective inquiry as a method for the acquisition of thinking skills implies the acceptance of the provisionality of human meaning and the continuous participation by learners in the process of meaning reconstruction. Equally, it recognizes that, as outlined by Dewey, individuals interact with their social environment, that is the school in our case, in testing and evaluating their interpretation of reality and for evaluating their judgements and decisions. For that reason alone, great care needs to be taken in the construction of the instructional (and institutional) environment for the development of critical and reflective thinking; the topic of the next section of this chapter.

Critical and reflective thinking

The roots of the approaches which were developed in the period after the Second World War to classroom practice for critical and reflective thinking are to be found in the work of pragmatist educational philosophy. Often referred to as critical inquiry, such approaches were developed by a group of North American social studies educators, such as Hullfish and Smith, Metcalf and Hunt, Meux and Combs, Engle, Oliver and Shaver, and Massialas. Drawing on the work of Dewey to a greater or lesser extent, the aim of all these writers was to facilitate induction of students to adult citizenship through various techniques of critical thinking, including hypothesis-testing, value-analysis, improvement of classroom discourse and question-and-answer techniques, including the grounding of correct answers, simulation of decision-making across significant social issues, and synthesizing information, principles and values to solve problems and propose policies.[34] Practical approaches to the development of critical thinking have been developed through the analysis of statistics, the recognition of valid generalizations, the search for and discovery of cause-and-effect relationships, distinguishing between relevant and irrelevant information, testing out the consistency of points of view, the development of the skills of inference drawing from known facts.[35] More recently, an attempt has been made to link together critical thinking, reflective thinking and inquiry and to define their roles in facilitating thinking in the social context.[36]

Another way of developing reflective inquiry and the skills of critical thinking is through the use of simulation. In a review article, published in the mid-1980s, White summarized the evidence on the use of simulation games as an instructional strategy which draws on reflective thinking and develops decision-making. He indicates that the research done so far is unsatisfactory, partly because of inadequate research design and methodology, but points out that there is evidence of positive effects in the affective domain as regards political attitudes. Slightly amending his conclusions, it is clear that simulation games, to be effective, must be standardized and workable, clearly identifying the objectives, structure and level of sophistication, subject matter, complexity of tasks and variety of interaction required of participants. They should be adequate models of social reality, commencing with situations which are relatively well known to the students.[37]

One technique which has been extensively used in social studies and law-related education is mock trials. Children's natural enjoyment of play-acting, combined with the television vogue for trial scenes, can be used to develop the capacity of students to see both sides of an argument. Preparation, including acting out familiar roles and establishing the roles and rules of the game, is of course necessary, as well as training in such skills as mediation and negotiation. It is also essential to talk out the activity at the end so that it is quite clear that roles played during simulation are play roles and not to be carried over into real life.[38]

A similar function may be fulfilled by case studies, and indeed some authors concentrate almost exclusively on the latter as the best means to achieve better decision-making and critical thinking.[39] A further way in which critical and reflexive thinking can be fostered is through the use of information technology. The whole cycle of deciding what information is required, searching for the information, selecting the resources, retrieving the information, processing it, recording it, reviewing it, presenting it and evaluating the completion of the task is a useful way of nurturing skills of observation, analysis, questioning, organizing, interpreting, hypothesis formulation, synthesizing, interpreting and communicating, such as are at the base of being logical, rational, systematic and self-critical.[40] The acquisition of information-processing skills therefore has an important contribution to the development of critical and reflective thinking.

Knowledge and expertise of the democratic process

One of the most effective ways of developing a commitment to the democratic process in students is by giving them opportunities to model and practise some of the basic principles of democracy. Cooperation and sharing of responsibility is one way. Another is direct experience, for example in community service or participation in school democracy, or indirect experience through such techniques as mock trials or mock parliamentary procedures. A third would be through the combination of social with scientific interests. One development in the United States, which appears to have spurred a new interest in combining social and scientific interests among children, is the so-called STS (science–technology–society) education. It is claimed that this approach stimulates curiosity, improves attitudes (including attitudes to the teacher's role as facilitator), develops skills of questioning and of perceiving cause and effect, and encourages students to become involved in resolving social issues.[41]

In Australia the concept of education for active citizenship has grown in importance in the late 1980s and early 1990s. Here two goals are emphasized: students' knowledge of society and the empowerment of students to participate effectively in society. In a survey of current approaches in Australian schools, a recent publication gives numerous examples of the ways in which schools and education systems are currently seeking to develop those qualities of active participation which are required by modern pluralist societies, not least by encouraging students to test out the congruence between democratic ideals and school realities. A new organization, established in 1989 and entitled the Australian Association of Parliamentary and Citizenship Education, promotes these ideas in various ways, including through the training of teachers.[42]

There is a particularly large literature concerned with cooperative group work in the classroom. In an evaluation of different cooperative approaches to learning, Herz-Lazarowitz has recently postulated that there are six basic interactive dimensions in communication in each classroom: classroom organization; structure of the learning task; teacher's communication; instructional style; students' academic behaviour; and students' social behaviour.[43] She points out that, of the six dimensions, relatively little work has been done on the impact of the structure of the learning task and of teachers' communication styles on the quality of cooperation and learning in the classroom, and she proposed that the style of cooperation, whether about product (informative), process (applicative) or means (evaluative), will influence the level of elaboration of the cooperation which takes place. Her tentative conclusion, that cooperation about means will produce higher level elaboration, has fundamental implications for the design of classroom learning contexts and strategies for global citizenship education.

Thus, depending on the developmental level of the students and their experience in cooperative modes of learning, teachers need to take into account all three media for cooperation, gradually increasing the emphasis on cooperation about means with the increasing age and growing maturity of the students. This may involve greater emphasis on open-ended tasks, greater autonomy on the part of students in generating their own cooperative tasks, and less close monitoring by the teacher of the objectives, content and process of cooperative work. All of these imply a greater emphasis on students taking responsibility for not only their own learning but also that of their peers.

Given such approaches on the part of the teacher, learning interactions which are characterized by peer collaboration or cooperative group methods can also be characterized by high levels of mutuality and equality, two of the core values of global citizenship education. These methods also encourage children to reason, to solve problems and to engage in the social exchange of ideas, which are likely to address others of the values, such as due process, participation and social responsibility. They are certainly well disposed to enhance the master value commitment of respect for persons, and to encourage not only the statement of such values, but also the active social demonstration of them. They therefore facilitate those qualities of understanding, integrity, communicative competence and ability to marshall rational arguments, as well as a commitment to the rule of law, which are at the heart of an equally just society, school and learning process. Educators need to review such recent writing and research, which has highlighted those collaborative and cooperative approaches that are capable of encouraging the child's active participation within a carefully and sensitively structured instructional context and thus foster high interactive mutuality.[44]

Turning now to community service, we find that there are a number of caveats. Firstly, strong support is necessary from school administration and staff, including the principal. Secondly, goals should be sharply defined and should be achievable and realistic. Clearly, what is realistic depends on the age of the children and the form of the activity proposed. Quite young children may be involved in community service, in groups and with direct supervision of teachers, but by and large citizenship practice in the early years will be predominantly in the sheltered atmosphere of the school and classroom. Thirdly, some training may be necessary both for teachers and students. Fourthly, one must make plans *re* foreseeable obstacles and problems. Fifthly, the work should include opportunities for students to reflect on their experiences. Sixthly, the work should be integrated with the ongoing work in the schools and related to the children's interests. And finally, there should be some form of reward or reinforcement for what has been learned.[45]

Attentiveness to developmental approaches

In spite of the work of the Early Childhood Advisory Board of the National Council for the Social Studies in the United States,[46] there is still a dearth of material about the opportunities for citizenship education in the early years. Yet it is important to note the early stage of human development at which prejudice, ethnic bigotry and gender bias may be learned as part of a stereotyping process beginning at birth and based on false or inappropriate generalization and dichotomous thinking.[47] There is no doubt also that socialization into one's own culture may predispose one to judge other cultures in a negative way.

In an attempt to develop a longitudinal approach to education for citizenship and one which is attentive to the developmental stages to which any citizenship education has to respond, recent work by Dynneson and Gross, quoted in outline in the last chapter, has attempted to construct a six-phase theoretical model for citizenship education, matched to the developmental levels of children and their social development.[48]

In that model the first stage is that of what is termed *biological citizenship*, where the child is almost totally dependent for its social relationships as for all else on its mother. This is an important stage for the beginnings of generalizations and attributions, as in the case of lightness and darkness and colour, and for the consideration of the extent to which the rhymes, jingles, songs and fairy tales of early childhood education may be considered to reinforce or inhibit cultural openness and healthy social relationships. It is also a time when the child understands that one does not hurt that which one loves, and begins to exercise responsibility for itself and its belongings.

Similarly, in the second stage of *family citizenship*, where the child's social world expands to include a wider circle of family and friends, some of the child's values and assumptions will be challenged, others reinforced. We know that through these first two stages the child acquires values and attitudes which will be very difficult but not impossible to change later. The onus on educators in the preschool phase is to work for the eradication of those early prejudices and, conversely, for promoting the values and skills of social association and judgement, for the early years are a time when citizenship concepts such as justice or fair play begin to develop in children and can thus be fostered through the right kind of activity[49] as part of an ongoing and coherent experience throughout the school life of the child.[50]

Early work in prenumeracy and preliteracy is well suported by a child-centred classroom which nurtures inquiry, the generation of ideas, cooperation and a sense of belonging and learning by doing, so that children generate their own knowledge and in particular their own attitudes to human association.[51] But teachers need to facilitate the process by providing materials and situations which are at least in part familiar to the children, so that they can incorporate new knowledge into existing schemata.[52] Concepts of privacy and honesty become more developed at this stage, although regression is not unusual and appropriate behaviour should be gently shaped and reinforced. Then, too, teachers must gradually expand the areas over which children have responsibility, introducing the idea of being responsible for others.

The third stage is that of *non-biological social relationships*, where the child comes into contact with peers outside the family, and ultimately in the school. Here the first scientific approaches to categorization and generalization occur for most children, through such work as setting in mathematics and the classification of physical objects in similar or identical groups. Reception-class teachers have the opportunity and power to work mightily for cooperative citizenship and the recognition of rights and responsibilities, as well as against prejudice and stereotypical representation. Here pupils may learn about rules of the school and personal behaviour in a sympathetic and supportive ambience. Fairness will be a dimension of the child's experience, both in its own right and as a precursor to issues of justice, mutuality and reciprocity. Young children like putting themselves into the position of others, they like role-playing and games. They like taking responsibility for tidying the play house or the reading corner or the science table. They like hearing stories of moral virtue and replicating that virtue in written or other media. But they also need to begin to learn that any human association means losing some of one's autonomy and individuality. It implies learning to share and learning to give.

The fourth phase is that of *stratified social citizenship*, where the development of social categorization is strengthened and membership behaviour grows. This is clearly a crucial stage for the development of concepts of cooperative citizenship as also for the development or eradication of prejudiced or stereotypical views of other people, their cultural values and mores, their appearance, ethnicity and nationality. At this stage, in-group/out-group behaviour strengthens and pupils deepen their appreciation of rules and norms of social association, and begin to understand and demonstrate their role in conflict resolution and in protecting members from antisocial behaviour and unhappiness. Equally, pupils may begin to understand and practice the rules of procedure, whereby rules may be changed or legitimated by rational discourse. The appreciation of each individual's human rights may be strengthened, including the right to dissent; but pupils may also come to realize that the interface of collective human rights may limit those of the individual. The engagement with the concept and practice of fairness and justice may continue and broaden into concepts of equal national and international justice. All the time, the concept of moral progression should be emphasizing the gradual maturing of individual autonomy combined with social responsiveness and accountability.

At the penultimate level, in stage five, predominantly horizontal social relationships develop as part of a period of *horizontally expanded citizenship*, where peer-group relationships exert extraordinarily strong influence. This occurs in early adolescence, and is the crucial time for developing autonomous, but socially responsible, citizenship. If early moral autopilot were ever crucial, it is during this phase. Educators must be aware of this and act accordingly. Teachers must provide environments in which pupils can reflectively develop their own values and participate in the positive change of their own social environment. Law-related education becomes more pronounced, as does a knowledge of the functioning of the legal and political systems. The reasons for and utility of the rule of law at local national and international levels also becomes more important and responsibility for other people takes on a wider connotation, as through the adoption of a prisoner of conscience or partner school in a developing country. Issues of cultural diversity and the conflicts and dilemmas inherent within pluralist societies come to the forefront, and community service and sharing take on greater importance.

Finally, there is the stage of *vertically expanded citizenship*, where new group social relationships are developed, and the search commences for stability between and within groups; a time of search for social order and structure among groups. This is essentially a period of consolidation before the launching into adult life and it must seek to build on the gains of the earlier years. Students may learn about the exercise of rights and responsibilities through the legal framework and the distinction between moral, customary and legal norms and the way in which each of these domains of norms acts differentially on human behaviour and impacts on the concept of justice. The ideas of responsible consumerism and local, national and international good neighbourliness and environmental stewardship require matching with the interrelationship of local, national and international laws, convention and agreements. At this stage basic knowledge of other countries' systems and approaches may be utilized to develop critical discourse on the home-base system and its effectiveness. Students should learn that countries, even democratic ones, sometimes infringe the rights of their citizens and that there are means to make sure that they do not do that with impunity and to ensure redress of those wrongs. They should learn something of the means whereby nations may seek redress against each other and of the various international instruments for human rights and justice.

These six stages all have their own demands in terms of educational strategies, which educators need to take into account in the design and delivery of global citizenship education. They represent a gradually broadening wedge of responsibility and appreciation of human rights, their function and implementation. All educators, at whatever level, must give attention to the development of the appropriate skills; but, clearly, the level of development of the child will make a difference to the sophistication of the approach and the selection of content.[53]

Commitment to human rights and social responsibilities

In spite of the relatively immature nature of the consideration of the educational implications of the development of an *active commitment to human rights and social responsibilities*, there is increasing recognition of its importance and new instructional materials are now beginning to emerge.[54] It has been suggested, and it is the view of this writer, that human rights education is a conscious strategy to make students aware of their human rights and social responsibilities, to sensitize them to the rights of others, and to encourage responsible action to secure the rights of all.[55] This tripartite definition usefully alerts us to the permeative nature of human rights and the fact that they are not static but are constantly expanding, so that their educational implications need to be continually reworked.

Human rights provide the moral core and basic norms for those free associations of human beings which rest on a greater common interest than self-interest. They are the basis for a normative affective paradigm of human nature and the social construction of a more just reality at the three levels and across all the domains of knowledge proposed in this book. They are the ethical fulcrum for the kind of global citizenship education, being advocated in this book, which is seen as part of the basic moral education of all students for the whole of their lives, in school and out, during school and in their adult years. They provide the values for the content, structure and process of all education at all levels and in all modes. They are, at the same time, part of the content of education and the provider of the criteria by which decisions about education are validated and legitimated. They thus provide ethical guidelines for the organization of education, internationally, nationally, institutionally and instructionally in all dimensions: aims and intentions, content, procedures and processes, assessment and evaluation.[56] They cannot be the preserve of any one subject of the curriculum exclusively.

But teaching of and for human rights in school can be an arid and abstract enterprise, and for that reason it is important for teachers to design activity approaches, some of which reach out beyond the school or classroom. Some schools, for example, have adopted a prisoner of conscience, while others have twinned with a school in a developing country. In some cases intervisiting of staff and students has been arranged. Some teachers use role-playing, simulation, drama, case histories and mock trials and broader themes from law-related education, such as consumer law, which can be made very topical and interesting.[57] Perhaps one of the most effective ways of introducing students to demonstrated commitments to human rights is by building them into the relationships within the school and of the school with parents and the community.[58]

The obverse of the commitment of global citizenship education for human rights, justice and social responsibility, is the so-called 'rule of law'. There is often a task to be undertaken of moving children from a perception of the law as restrictive and punitive to a perception where they see the law as facilitative, promotive, comprehensible and alterable.[59] With regard to the content of this aspect of human rights and responsibilities, care needs to be taken not to produce an arid list of topics which may be beyond the grasp of the developmental stage of the children concerned. Certainly, by the end of compulsory schooling, students should know about what law is, the different categories of law, who makes law and how the adversary system works. They should also encounter explanations of the pathology of crime and come to understand that laws in pluralist societies are not always uncontroversial. Alongside their increasing economic awareness, they have to be aware of the way in which law protects their rights and those of others, not least as consumers in a market economy. Moreover, they need to understand the link in a democratic society between law and freedom, including the freedom of expression and protest, religion and peaceful assembly, which constitute cornerstones of democratic government. They need to know of the way in which the law impinges on the family and the rights of different members of the family. Not least they must realize the way in which the law combats discrimination and infringement of personal privacy.[60]

But what educational approaches are most efficient and cost effective at the classroom and individual levels? As suggested above, the effective schools movement in the United States and similar developments elsewhere have indicated the educational inputs which are likely to be most influential in stimulating learning. At the school and classroom level we also have catalogues of approaches which are known to be effective for cognitive and/or affective objectives. Often such methods are based on cooperative approaches to teaching and learning, including more democratic, values-oriented methods which appeal to the judgement of the learners.[61] Often they imply the pre-existence of democratic schools and classrooms.[62] A resume of such criteria, adapted to the goals of a more global citizenship education, might include the following:

(a) a democratic classroom ethos, engendering feelings of trust among pupils and between teachers and pupils;
(b) maximal use of collaborative and cooperative approaches;
(c) activity methods, including simulation, role-playing and varied group composition;
(d) utilization of rational methods, appealing to the judgement of the learners;
(e) support and assistance for pupils to evolve and clarify their own value systems;
(f) inclusion of situations involving value dilemmas;

(g) emphasis on open rather than closed questions;
(h) multiple approaches, including different media and locations and reinforcement regimes;
(i) inclusion of social responsibility and actioning;
(j) high intellectual expectation in both cognitive and affective domains;
(k) explicit commitment to human rights as the basis for all interaction in the classroom;
(l) linked, supportive assessment methods, oriented to student success.

World organizations, such as the World Bank, have begun to build on the work on effective schools, combining it with the results of work and research from the developing world to identify policies, approaches and inputs which can maximize learning cross-nationally. There is no reason why a similar approach should not be adopted towards global citizenship education.[63]

PROFESSIONAL DIALOGUE

This section is intended to encourage readers to take critical but principled distance from the principles and proposals advanced in this chapter, and, since they are the sequential result of the premises established in previous chapters, from the book as a whole.

(a) How would the lists of desirable characteristics at school and classroom levels need to be amended or amplified for your school and the classes you teach?
(b) In which ways is the effective schools research relevant to or explicatory of the approaches adopted by yourself and your colleagues to school organization and classroom teaching?
(c) How far do you think your school is able to deliver a democratic school and classroom ethos, engendering feelings of trust among pupils and between teachers and pupils?
(d) In which subject areas is it possible to maximize use of collaborative and cooperative approaches?
(e) In what ways can your own style of teaching accommodate more activity methods, including simulation, role-playing and varied student group composition?
(f) How far do your curriculum and assessment methods rely on the utilization of rational methods, appealing to the judgement of the learners?
(g) Is there support in all classes and processes, as well as assistance, for pupils to evolve and clarify their own value systems?
(h) Do you and does your curriculum encourage the inclusion of situations involving value dilemmas or do you tend to take the easy way by providing answers or easily soluble issues?
(i) In your teaching do you place an emphasis on open rather than closed questions?
(j) Do you use multiple approaches, including different media, locations and assessment strategies?

(k)   How far is it possible to include practical social responsibility and citizen actioning in your work?

(l)   Does your school maintain high intellectual expectation in both cognitive and affective domains?

(m)   Does the school have an explicit commitment to human rights as the basis for all interaction in the classroom?

(n)   Does the philosophy of teaching for the school include linked, supportive assessment methods, oriented to student success?

NOTES AND REFERENCES

1.   See Cherryholmes, C.H. (1990) *Political Scientists on Civic Education: A Non-Existent Discourse* (East Lansing, MI: Center for Learning and Teaching of Elementary Subjects, Michigan State University, Institute for Research on Teaching).

2.   Butts, R.F. (1980) *The Revival of Civic Learning* (Bloomington, IN: Phi Delta Kappa Educational Foundation).

3.   An interesting, if brief and limited, study of the 'appearance' of the decalogue of values in actual classroom practice is contained in Hodge, R.L. (1990) 'Middle school citizenship education: a study of civic values via R. Freeman Butts decalogue', paper presented at the Annual Conference of the American Educational Research Association, Boston, MA, 16-20 April.

4.   A recent article which critiques the historical development of social theory from Marx, Durkheim and Weber and the movement towards human ecology is Buttel, F.H. (1986) 'Sociology and the environment: the winding road towards human ecology', *International Journal of Educational Research*, **38**(3), 337-56.

5.   See Rawls, J. (1971) *A Theory of Justice* (Cambridge, MA: Harvard University Press).

6.   See Nisbett, R. and Ross, L. (1980) *Human Inference* (Englewood Cliffs, NJ: Prentice-Hall); and Guskey, T. (1986) 'Staff development and the process of teacher change', *Educational Researcher*, **15**(5), 5-12.

7.   MacIntyre, A. (1981) *After Virtue* (Notre Dame, IN: University of Notre Dame Press).

8.   For a discussion of the ethical preparation of educators, see Strike, K.A. (1990) 'Teaching ethics to teachers: what the curriculum should be about', *Teaching and Teacher Education*, **6**(1), 47-53.

9.   Scheerens, J. and Creemers, B.P.M. (1989) 'Conceptualizing school effectiveness', *International Journal of Educational Research,* **13**(7), 691-706.

10.   Stake, R.E. (1990) 'Situational context as influence on evaluation design and use', *Studies in Educational Evaluation,* **16**, 231-46.

11.   See, for example, Erickson, F. (1986) 'Qualitative methods in research on teaching', in M.C. Wittrock (ed.), *Handbook of Research on Teaching*, 3rd edn (New York: Macmillan).

12.   Wolcott, H. (1976) 'Criteria for an ethnographic approach to research in schools', in T.J. Roberts and S.K. Akinsanya (eds), *Schooling in the Cultural Context* (New York: David McKay).

13.   Walberg, H.J. (1986) 'Synthesis of research on teaching', in M.C. Wittrock (ed.), *Handbook of Research on Teaching*, 3rd edn. (Washington, DC: American Educational Research Association).

14.   Fraser, B.J., Walberg, H.J. Welch, W.W. and Hattie, J.A. (1987) 'Syntheses of educational productivity research', *International Journal of Educational Research,* **11**, 145-252.

15.   Fraser, B.J. (1989) 'Twenty years of classroom environment work: progress and prospect', *Journal of Curriculum Studies*.

16.   Fraser, B.J. (1989) 'Research synthesis on school and instructional effectiveness', *International Journal of Educational Research,* **13**(7), 707-19.

17. Kyle, R. A. (1985) *Reaching for Excellence: An Effective School Source Book* (Washington, DC: United States Government Printing Office).
18. Her Majesty's Inspectors of Schools (1977) *Ten Good Schools* (London: HMSO).
19. Rutter, M., Maughan, B., Mortimore, P. and Ouston, J. (1979) *Fifteen Thousand Hours: Secondary Schools and Their Effects on Children* (London: Open Books).
20. Lightfoot, S.L. (1983) *The Good High School* (New York: Basic Books).
21. I have collated a great deal of the literature in an earlier publication. See Lynch, J. (1987) *Prejudice Reduction and the Schools* (London: Cassell), especially Ch. 4.
22. See, for example, National Curriculum Council, *Education for Citizenship* (York: National Curriculum Council).
23. Raths, L.E., Harmin, M. and Simon, S.B. (1966) *Values and Teaching* (Columbus, OH: Charles E. Merrill).
24. For a useful overview of the material at that time, see Superka, D.P., Ahrens, C., Hedstrom, J.E. with Ford, L.J. and Johnson, P.L. (1976) *Values Education Source Book: Conceptual Approaches, Materials, Analyses, and an Annotated Bibliography* (Boulder, CO: ERIC Clearing House for Social Studies/Social Science Education).
25. Banks, J.A. (1985) *Teaching Strategies for the Social Studies*, 3rd edn (New York: Longman).
26. Kohlberg, L. (1981) *The Philosophy of Moral Development. Vol. 1: Development* (San Francisco, CA: Harper & Row).
27. Arbuthnot, J.B. and Faust, D. (1981) *Teaching Moral Reasoning: Theory and Practice* (New York: Harper & Row).
28. Metcalf, L. (1971) *Values Education* (Washington, DC: National Council for the Social Studies); and Kehoe, J.W. and Todd, R.W. (1978) 'Demonstrating the relationship between values and attitudes as a means of changing attitudes', *Alberta Journal of Educational Research*, 21(3), 207–12.
29. Kehoe, J.W. (1984) *A Handbook for Enhancing the Multicultural Climate of the School* (Vancouver, BC: Western Education Development Group, Faculty of Education, University of British Columbia).
30. Shaver, P. and Strong, W. (1982) *Facing Value Decisions: Rationale Building for Teachers* (New York: Teachers' College Press, Columbia University); and Strike, K.A. and Soltis, J.F. (1985) *The Ethics of Teaching* (New York: Teachers' College Press, Columbia University).
31. Flanagan, O.J. (1984) *The Science of Mind* (Cambridge, MA: MIT Press).
32. Mitsakos, C.L. (1978) 'A global education program can make a difference', *Theory and Research in Social Education*, 6, 1–15.
33. Eyler, J. (1981) 'Citizenship education for conflict: an empirical assessment of the relationship between principled thinking and tolerance for conflict and diversity', *Theory and Research in Social Education*, 8, 11–26.
34. Among the most important and influential texts of that period were: Hullfish, H.G. and Smith, P.G. (1961) *Reflective Thinking: The Method of Education* (New York: Dodd Mead); Hunt, M.P. and Metcalf, M.E. (1955) *Teaching High School Social Studies* (New York: Harper & Row); Metcalf, L.E. (1963) 'Research on teaching the social studies', in N.L. Gage (ed.), *Handbook of Research on Teaching*. Chicago: Rand McNally, pp. 929–65; Oliver, D.W. and Shaver, J.P. (1966) *Teaching Public Issues in the High School* (Boston: Houghton Mifflin); and Massialas, B.G. and Hurst, J.B. (1978) *Social Studies in a New Era. The School as a Laboratory for Real Life Experiences* (New York: Longman).
35. See, for example, Rudin, B. (1984) 'Teaching critical thinking skills', *Social Education*, 48(4), 279–81.
36. Brandhorst, A. and Splittgerber, F. (1987) 'Social studies and the development of thinking: the state of the art', *Southern Social Studies Quarterly*, 13(2), 20–42.
37. White, C.S. (1985) 'Citizen decision-making, reflective thinking and simulation gaming: a marriage of purpose, method and strategy', *Journal of Social Studies Research*, 2 (Summer), 1–50.
38. Hickey, M.G. (1990) 'Mock trials for children', *Social Education*, 54(1), 43–4.

39. Oliver, D. W. and Shaver, D. P. (1966) *Teaching Public Issues in the High School* (Boston: Houghton Mifflin).
40. A useful typology of the interrelationship of information skills and cross curriculum permeation is contained in National Council for Educational Technology (1989) *Information Skills and the National Curriculum* (Coventry: University of Warwick).
41. For a summary of the research evidence in this field, see Rubba, P. A. (1990) 'STS education in action: what researchers say to teachers', *Social Education,* 54(4), 201–3.
42. See, for example, the journal of the Association, *The Citizenship Educator*, and an article in its first issue: Glodman, J. and Russell, N. (1990) 'Participatory citizenship education: a continuing challenge for teacher educators', *The Citizenship Educator*, 1(1), 27–38. See also the survey in Parliament of the Commonwealth of Australia, Senate Standing Committee on Employment, Education and Training (1991) *Active Citizenship Revisited* (Canberra: The Publications Unit, Department of the Senate), pp. 9–39.
43. Hertz-Lazarowitz, R. (1989) 'Cooperation and helping in the classroom: a contextual approach', *International Journal of Educational Research*, 13(1), 113–19.
44. Damon, W. and Phelps, E. (1989) 'Critical distinctions among three approaches to peer education', *International Journal of Educational Research*, 13(1), 9–19.
45. For a list of such principles, see Reische, D. L. (1987) *Citizenship: Goal of Education* (Arlington, VA: American Association of School Administrators), especially Ch. 5.
46. Early Childhood Advisory Board, National Council for the Social Studies (1983) *Publicizing and Encouraging Elementary Social Studies: Strategies for State and Local Councils* (Washington, DC: National Council for the Social Studies).
47. Goodman, M. E. (1973) *Race Awareness in Young Children* (New York: Collier Books).
48. See Dynneson, T. L. and Gross, R. E. (1985) 'An eclectic approach to citizenship: developmental stages', *The Social Studies*, 76(1), 23–7.
49. Wright, I. (1988) 'Citizenship education and decision-making', *International Journal of Social Education*, 3(2), 55–62.
50. For example, Kneedler, P. E. (1988) 'Assessment of critical thinking skills in history/social science', *Social Studies Review*, 27(3), 2–93.
51. Piaget, J. (1963) *The Child's Conception of the World* (Patterson, NJ: Littlefield Adams); and (1971) *Psychology and Epistemology* (New York: Grossman).
52. An article which contains a number of suggestions for an early-years approach to citizenship is McGowan, T. M. and Godwin, C. M. (1986) 'Citizenship in the early grades: a plan for action', *The Social Studies*, September/October, 196–200.
53. For an example of progression and continuity in the development of one curriculum on citizenship, on which the above has drawn, see National Curriculum Council (1990) *Education for Citizenship* (York: National Curriculum Council), pp. 18–19.
54. See, for example, Starkey, H. (1988) 'Practical activities for teaching and learning about human rights in schools'. Oxford: Westminster College.
55. Tarrow, N. B. (1988) *Human Rights and Education* (Oxford: Pergamon).
56. I have utilized a similar definition in a previous publication: see Lynch, J. (1989) *Multicultural Education in a Global Society* (London: Falmer Press), p. 81.
57. For younger children, see Alonzo, J. R. and Jenkins, J. (1989) 'Law in Toyland', *Update on Law-related Education*, Winter, 9–10; and, for older children, Gallagher, A. F. (1989) 'Access to justice', *Update on Law-related Education*, Winter, as examples of the kind of material which is now becoming available. An example of an approach using consumer law is Bjiorklun, E. C. (1989) 'Teaching about consumer law: activities for the classroom', *The Social Studies*, 80(6), 240–5.
58. Ray, D. and D'Oyley, V. (1983) *Human Rights in Canadian Education* (Dubuque, IA: Kendall Hunt).
59. A useful critical learning outcomes continuum for law-related education is Anderson, C. C. (1990) 'Promoting responsible citizenship through elementary law-related education', *Social Education*, 44(5), 383–6.
60. A lay approach to many of these topics, which provides a useful conceptual framework for

content selection, is McMahon, E. T., Arbetman, P. E. and O'Brien, E. L. (1986) *Street Law* (St Paul, MN: West Publishing).

61. Slavin, R. E. (1985) *Learning to Cooperate: Cooperating to Learn* (New York: Plenum Press).

62. Gutmann, A. (1987) *Democratic Education* (Princeton, NJ: Princeton University Press).

63. Lockheed, M. E. and Verspoor, A. M. (1990) *Improving Primary Education in Developing Countries* (Washington, DC: World Bank).

Chapter 5

Assessing and Evaluating

INTRODUCTION

This chapter, holding faithful to the overall principles of procedure for the book defined in the Introduction, addresses issues of the assessment of students, the self-appraisal of teachers and the evaluation of programme and institutional practices for global citizenship education. The chapter commences by relating the discussion of the evaluation of global citizenship education to the literature of evaluation more generally. It raises the basic issues of institutional evaluation in the form of ten fundamental questions about institutions committed to the principles of global citizenship education. The chapter then continues with a consideration of what factors might inhibit the introduction of programmes of global citizenship education, so that institutions can plan evaluation, professional appraisal and student assessment strategies which facilitate rather than impede appropriate educational change.

The chapter suggests an overall approach which maximizes the background ideological values and beliefs which inform teachers' professional practice. By this means, teachers' and students' values, attitudes and knowledge and those of the reformed institutional ethos may be gradually brought together so that there is ever greater congruence of theories and practice, and of institutional goals and behaviour. This shift in the base-values paradigm of the institution should then become gradually manifest in its curricula, teaching/learning methods, structure, policy and procedures, including communication within the institution and with the surrounding community.

The chapter then raises the issue of the mechanisms through which school, programme and educator performance for global citizenship education and its classroom curriculum may be monitored and evaluated and how the cognitive, affective and behavioural learning of students may be assessed and judged, across the three levels of citizenship advocated in this book and pertaining to all the domains of knowledge. The chapter advocates a high measure of both institutional and professional self-evaluation, without neglecting the dilemma of reconciling such an 'autonomous' approach with three basic considerations: the need for democratic accountability, the requirements of an emancipatory concept of citizenship, and the dangers of 'cultural and moral inbreeding' by developing a closed cycle of institutional and professional orthodoxy.

The pursuit of equal social justice based on the recognition of everyone's human rights and interfaced social responsibilities is paramount in setting criteria for evaluation and professional judgement, whether about the institution, its goals and programmes, teachers' professional performance or the achievement and behaviour of students. Emphasis is placed on the need to decide and to act on rational judgements, which manifest respect for persons, due process, mutuality and reciprocity among all members of the school community, as well as with the wider national and international community. Equally, however, it is important that such decisions are developmental, in the sense that they are themselves responsive to criteria of democratic pluralism, the body of human rights covenants and the gradually enlarging human perception and practice of human rights and democracy. Thus the very principles of mutuality, reciprocity and reversibility of judgements and decisions are not based on a 'static', but on the gradual passage of humankind along the 'human rights developmental stages', as the meaning of human rights, the boundaries of how we perceive and understand freedoms and justice are gradually expanded and, at the same time, extended to all humans.

In this chapter, I propose detailed criteria for institutional and programme evaluation, for staff appraisal and for student assessment. I suggest strategies for dealing humanely with deficits and putting them right, and for handling the problem of recalcitrance. Once again, the principles of procedure for the book as a whole are adhered to and proposals are negotiated with the reader on a dialogical basis, rather than being presented as *ex cathedra* proposals. Again too, everything that is suggested is provisional, and educators are invited to take issue with what is proposed.

BASIC ISSUES OF EVALUATION

There are basically five different but interrelated kinds of evaluation: institutional evaluation; programme or curriculum evaluation; personnel evaluation; product evaluation; and policy evaluation. In this chapter, while we shall be concerned with all five, we shall focus predominantly on institutional and programme/curriculum evaluation; personnel evaluation, which we shall refer to as professional appraisal; and the evaluation of students (not explicitly one of the above five), which we shall refer to as student assessment.

Throughout this book, I have emphasized the need for teachers to be what the Carnegie Foundation calls reflective and thoughtful professionals.[1] They must engage with ends as well as means, with reasons and justifications as much as with techniques, and with the rationales for their professional actions and judgements as much as the way they deliver someone else's package. This implies looking at the underlying assumptions and values of teaching and learning and, of course, the ends and ways in which those assumptions and values and the programmes which absorb and build on them are evaluated. In terms of the curriculum, it involves curriculum analysis and both summative and formative curriculum evaluation.[2] It also implies asking questions about the reasons for evaluation and the purposes to which the products of evaluation are intended to be applied. Such principles fit with an emancipatory concept of global citizenship education, which is not the unquestioning slave of the social, political and economic purposes of dominant groups, as well as with the overarching goal of such programmes, which is the education of humane, sensitive and responsible members of communities, countries and the world, who are committed to democracy and the human rights of all.

Sometimes, however, the process of evaluation is perceived or designed in a way which is discordant with the above ideals. It may be perceived merely as a mechanism of control for educational bureaucracies, calculated to hold professionals and students in intellectual thraldom, to provide for the appearance of responsibility rather than its essence, to restrict the horizon across which human rights may be seen as applicable. Consequently, it is often regarded by teachers as a threat to them rather than as an opportunity for their own professional growth and increased job satisfaction, and by students as just another example of the gap between declared and operative values. On the other hand and at the other end of the spectrum, some argue the need for an often undefined maximum of professional autonomy, if teachers are to make the evaluation mode their own and thus to fulfil a major dimension of being a reflective professional, an essential prerequisite to producing reflective students and future citizens.

There is clearly a dilemma to be resolved along the continuum from teacher self-evaluation to bureaucratic teacher-evaluation, and different systems and different institutions will resolve that dilemma in different ways. By analogy, there is a similar continuum between autonomy and control for institutional evaluation and student assessment. Absolute autonomy or absolute control are not humanly viable models of evaluation, and the locus of evaluation along the continuum needs to be based on the values and principles of global citizenship education.

A situation of alienation or even downright rejection often arises because there has been no clarity in defining the kind of evaluation and its location along the continuum, on the use to which the evaluation is to be applied, or because the process of dialogue has been deficient. In some cases, for example, because the views of teachers are neither solicited nor valued, the instruments, procedures and purposes proposed for the evaluation are not positively viewed by teachers.[3] Sometimes too the standards against which teachers (or schools and students) are being evaluated are none too clear or have grown up in an ad hoc way, which has reflected the 'urgent' demands of quality assurance and the kind of evaluative data that are most readily available.[4] Then too, the professional standards and criteria for evaluation are sometimes seen as purely those of the evaluators, and evaluators are often seen as separate from the professional task of teaching. Moreover, the data, when collected, is poorly communicated, so that the whole process is seen as a bureaucratic waste of time and in the interests neither of student nor teacher. Such policies are clearly professionally counterproductive and would, in any case, be out of line with the basic principles of a human-rights-based global citizenship education.

Before moving to a deeper consideration of the assessment of students, the appraisal of staff and the evaluation of schools and programmes, there are certain 'foundation' issues of the social and cultural purposes of evaluation, with which any overall evaluation of a school must concern itself. These social and cultural purposes concern not only the overall goals of evaluation but also the process of evaluation, and they provide a certain rationale for its design and implementation. It is useful to discuss those issues within the context of the contemporary literature on educational evaluation, focusing on two basic aspects of that literature: the functional and professional utility of self-evaluation, and the need for both summative and formative evaluation interactively as part of a coherent mixed-method policy for institutional evaluation.[5]

IMPEDIMENTS TO EVALUATION FOR GLOBAL CITIZENSHIP EDUCATION

No innovation can assume a carte blanche. There are always pre-existing conditions and values, attitudes and professional beliefs, ideologies and implicit theories, which may stand in the way even of the most mild proposals for change, and such pre-existing conditions need to be taken seriously, if evaluation is to be useful, effective and personally and professionally satisfactory and developmental.[6] Yet change can and does happen and experience suggests that the direction of change can be influenced, even if it cannot be planned to the last detail. As pointed out in the last chapter, there are similarly conditions and values which will facilitate the achievement of the desired goal. This holds good particularly where there is already a good ethos, sense of school community and shared values and good relationships with parents, so that even the most seemingly intractable problems and the most apparently threatening of changes can be addressed in an atmosphere of mutual respect, drawing on an overall code of conduct for human relations, which is congruent with the values of the formal and informal curriculum. The innovation proposed in this book may be radical for many schools, but it may find a good seedbed in the already existing relationships within the school.

The art of innovation is to be able to recognize which are the benevolent pre-existing conditions and to introduce the change in such a way as to hook onto those and to obviate or mitigate the inimical factors. Clearly, to maximize these former, there needs to be a dialogical approach within a non-threatening climate.[7] The dialogical, participatory approach is important if a sense of professional commitment and ownership is to be generated and bitterness, alienation and frustration at someone else's requirement are to be avoided.[8] Such a participatory approach needs to be based on 'professional respect for persons', which complements the overall professional and cultural ethos of a school and its commitment to basic human rights.[9] It should also be closely related to the professional practice of the teacher, so that the teacher can define his or her own needs and take ownership of both problem definition and resolution.

For such a climate to be fostered, teachers' pre-existing values and professional assumptions and theories must be taken into account. Recent research has indicated once again the close relationship between teachers' beliefs about specific educational practices and the quality of implementation of new instructional practices.[10] More recently attempts have been made to subject the rather vaguer and more hazy background ideological beliefs that teachers hold to a similar scrutiny, which indicates that these beliefs have considerable effect on three aspects: the planning and preparatory, implementational and decision-making, and monitoring and evaluative stages of teachers' own instruction.[11]

So the congruence between teachers' beliefs about education and their perception of, commitment to, and therefore effectiveness of, implementation of global citizenship education is a crucial variable in developing change strategies to introduce it. Moreover, since the goals of citizenship education, as we have seen in previous chapters, are predominantly personal and social, and since citizenship education is often spread throughout the curriculum or delegated to a relatively non-prestigious component of the curriculum, which may not even be legitimated by formal examinations or assessments, it follows that institutions and educators are likely to give less attention, energy and consideration to it than to academic goals.[12] Moreover, the aims of personal and social education, even where they are recognized as important, are often regarded as being means to achieve or to supplement academic goals, rather than as fully worthy goals in their own right. This academic hegemony is so strong that the introduction of a free-standing commitment by the institution or individual educator to broader social goals may arouse considerable conscious or unconscious, overt or covert, opposition, even where those goals are legitimated by authority.

One way to reconcile the need for a high level of congruence between teachers' ideological commitment to academic goals and their beliefs in the academic prowess of their institution with the need to develop global citizenship education with its heavily social and personal goals is, as suggested above, to focus on the instructional process. Such an approach can allow the innovation to demonstrate through appropriate classroom practice the improvement in students' learning outcomes and permit that, in turn, to alter teachers' beliefs and goal perceptions.[13] Moreover, since, as argued and illustrated in previous chapters, global citizenship education comprises a fundamental mass of content, concepts and basic analytical and problem-solving skills, and since both teachers and pupils gain their academic and social stature predominantly through the pursuit of academic goals, it is important to maximize these aspects of citizenship education to make it more congruent with the dominant values and belief systems of the institution and educator, that is, to emphasize the academic rigour of the pursuit of that goal. To empower students to achieve goals of values and expertise, in other words, they must be enabled to demonstrate them. Students' competence, for example, in curricular areas cited in the last chapter, such as the skills of inquiry, in the formulation and testing of hypotheses and the more general application of scientific inquiry techniques to issues, topics and problems and decision-making may be a means not only to the achievement of those goals, but also to the legitimation of the programme of global citizenship education.

Moreover, as pointed out in the last chapter, 'good' teachers will already have a generalized ideological commitment to many of the values inherent in global citizenship education, such as due process, respect for persons and privacy. Further, as argued in the last chapter, teachers can only fulfil their professional functions effectively if they adhere reasonably to those concepts and values which are at the base of global citizenship education. These values are part of the overall ideology of the teacher, influencing both the teacher's belief system and implicit professional theories, and through them the teacher's planning, decision-making and evaluation of his or her own professional performance.[14]

Values such as intellectual integrity are internal to the methods or practice of global citizenship education.[15] Assessment, for example, demands of teacher and taught acquaintance and acceptance of the concept of due process of fairness and of respect for rational evidence and balance. So there are pre-existing beliefs which can facilitate the achievement of our goals, and their evaluation, using strategies that emphasize those common core values and the instructional dimension, as well as the achievement of the students. Moreover, in concert with the 'teacher as researcher' movement of the 1960s and 1970s, such an approach enables change to be conceptualized as a bottom-up rather than top-down exercise, so that real commitment grows naturally from the activity of professional practice.[16] The design and delivery of this process is crucial, otherwise the result will be the appearance of success rather than the essence. For that reason, this chapter seeks to focus on the means whereby the instructional goals, and prior to them the institutional goals (see Chapters 3 and 4), may be assessed and evaluated.

Such a strategy does not imply that we shall neglect the point made in Chapter 4 that the contextual characteristics of educational endeavours are crucial in the construction of the common meanings underpinning the instructional enterprise.[17] They are also crucial to the development of an appropriately reflective and, therefore, reflexive practice, which uses the shared experience of the classroom (among teachers and between teachers and students) as a seedbed for considered educational and narrower instructional change. The more teachers can evaluate and innovate in their own professional practice, the more likely they are also to change their values and ideological beliefs and, thence, to engage for the change of their institution, its ethos, policies and practices, through an informed and educated democratic discourse from which coercion is alien. In this way democratic evaluation, and democratic assessment as a part of it, can become integral to the professional practice of each educator and each school.[18]

EMPOWERMENT FOR CITIZENSHIP EVALUATION

A number of writers have suggested that one way of overcoming professional or organizational fear of evaluation is to empower the institution and the professional to be self-evaluating. But, in a democratic society, there is never one person or one institution who is in a position to decide not only whether the school and the teacher are achieving their objectives, but also whether those objectives are the right ones. That process of defining goals for both institutions and programmes, as well as their evaluation, must always be a discourse between different groups and individuals. For the teacher or participants in the process, it has to be remembered that any evaluation involves putting themselves and their professional identity in an exposed position. Moreover, evaluation should be a process involving the renegotiation of teachers' own professional reality and the gradual extension of the criteria by which they judge their own performance, while recognizing, at the same time, the value and role of inputs from other interested parties both into goals and into means.

Thus no individual and no school within a pluralist democracy can be given total autonomy in the evaluation of its own performance. On the other hand, no evaluation is likely to extend and improve institutional performance unless it is professionally credible to that institution and its personnel and unless the personnel concerned are involved in a meaningful way in setting the goals, processes and principles of procedure for the evaluation. Thus, the self-evaluating institution is neither fully independent nor fully dominated by the will, the values and the controls of others, but it is subject to pressure from them on a heavily contested field of human endeavour.[19]

I have already stated that any evaluation for a more globally sensitive approach to citizenship education in schools, which is attentive to social responsibilities and human rights, must itself be attentive to those principles. It must take as its touchstone respect for persons, for the integrity of their personality, their human and professional sensitivity, their right to reasonable privacy and the need for due process. Evaluations, and particularly staff appraisals, must be wary of inadvertently setting up a kind of irrefutable inquisitional monster, which is cavalier with the rights of individuals and against which there is neither redress nor rectification. The provisionality of human judgement and its proneness to error and even injustice, its responsiveness to facile group consensus and pressure, need to be in the minds of those who develop and implement the strategy for evaluation in a school.

As set out in the classic literature on evaluation as long ago as 1942, the purposes of evaluation are seen as:

(a) to provide a periodic check on the effectiveness of the educational institution and to indicate the points at which improvements in the programme may be necessary;

(b) to validate the hypotheses upon which an educational institution's operation is based;

(c) to access information basic to effective guidance of individual students;

(d) to enhance the psychological well-being of the school community;

(e) to provide a sound basis for public relations.[20]

These stated purposes may have a somewhat old-fashioned ring, and they may need to be strengthened in terms of the evaluation of curricula and the role of that evaluation in the improvement of practice, but they are still a useful starting point for formulating an evaluation policy aimed at global citizenship education as part of the overall mission statement of the school. To follow Tyler's logic further, those purposes prompt us to ask questions about the extent to which the educational experiences, designed to achieve such purposes, have been organized, and how we can apprehend whether these educational purposes have been achieved and, if not, why not.

There are, of course, consequential questions about the use to which material accruing from the evaluation is put, and by what media the results of evaluation are disseminated. Looked at another way, the questions assume the existence of an implicit school covenant or explicit mission statement, which has been negotiated among the members of the school community, and a set of obligations, into which the school has entered, to deliver that mission statement and to achieve the inherent aims and objectives within it. They also concern the ways in which evidence may be found to substantiate a judgement about those issues, as well as the policies for remedy and amendment, institutionally and instructionally, with regard to content, process, structure and policy. Further, they raise the issue of how to use any 'findings' or results of evaluation to improve the relationship on which successful delivery of the school's programme depends.

Such a process rests upon the assumption that each school has a published mission statement, at the heart of which is a set of values which defines that school, including its evaluation policy, through a set of values and symbols, statements and shared experiences. The school's mission statement will differentiate the school from other similar institutions, emphasizing its individuality and uniqueness, while at the same time linking it in collegiality and commonality with all other similar institutions in a free, democratic and pluralist society and more broadly within a world context. That link will be based both on reciprocity and accountability to a community outside the school for social purposes based on the human rights of the individual but recognizing a social responsibility broader than that of the individual.

Three 'model' scenarios may perhaps be envisaged. In the first case, a school may have such a mission statement or promulgated commitment, which has remained unaltered and has been overtaken, so that it is a memorial to a structure of beliefs and commitments no longer relevant to its contemporary mission. In a second case, there may be no such statement and perhaps there never has been, except at an implicit level, and one needs to be constructed from scratch. In a third case, there may already be such a statement and, as part of the process of overall institutional evaluation, it is being reviewed against the values of the school and society.

In any of these three 'model' cases, certain overarching issues need to be raised in the context of the school's reflective dialogue with its purposes and their evaluation. Such issues might include the following:

(a) What are the school's overall mission, goals and objectives, and how congruent are they with the principles of human rights and social responsibilities at the three levels of citizenship identified in this book?

(b) How well negotiated, promulgated and disseminated are those goals and objectives with the various groups in the school community?

(c) What educational obligations has the school assumed to muster its resources to activate, state and demonstrate its commitment?

(d) Are such obligations appropriate to the school's location, facilities, human and material resources, and to the students, given their ages and stages of development?

(e) Are all the school's activities, programmes, reward systems and procedures consistent with its goals and objectives set out in its mission statement?

(f) Are the school's structure, staffing, communications, curricula and assessment policies, including for non-academic achievements, well designed to achieve the goals contained in its mission statement?

(g) What evidence is there that the school is achieving its goals or of why it is failing to achieve them?

(h) Is there a policy for human, physical and fiscal resources which would facilitate the achievement of the school's goals?

(i) Are the mechanisms and processes in place for participatory change by teachers, parents and pupils to more closely achieve the mission statement?

(j) Does the school offer and create opportunities for pupils of all ages to take on appropriate responsibilities?[21]

(k) What policies exist for addressing issues concerned with the environment of the school, the community and more broadly?

(l) Is law-related education a part of citizenship education? How effectively is it achieved and are there mechanisms for its continual updating?

(m) How effective are the policies and procedures for keeping all staff up to date with the development of citizenship education and their role in its delivery?

(n) What changes need to be made to more closely achieve the mission statement?[22]

(o) Are there previous evaluation case histories on which the current review could draw?[23]

Such questions serve a number of fundamental and essential purposes. They provide what Carol Weiss has called an 'illumination of the backdrop' against which the educational processes of institutional and programme evaluation, staff appraisal and student assessment take place.[24] They can produce a wealth of basic information about the context within which teaching and learning operate and the curriculum is delivered. They help to clarify the social and professional purposes of evaluation, the principles of procedure for such evaluations and, if previous evaluation 'case law' exists, they provide an historical profile or depth for the currently proposed evaluation. They are, in a sense, both intrinsic and extrinsic to the baseline review. They are part of the question of what educational purposes the school seeks to achieve, how it formulates those purposes in the form of a curriculum and how effectively it is achieving these purposes. Equally, they are the first external stimulants to the discourse about those purposes and their achievement. They are, in a sense, however, no more than rough-hewn starting points for the review of the institution and its programme which is essential if a school is to keep itself on contract with its mission statement and values, and if that statement and those values, in turn, are to be kept in tune with the basic principles of human rights and justice and social responsibilities.

EVALUATION, APPRAISAL AND ASSESSMENT

As indicated above, there are three aspects to the overall monitoring by a school of its effectiveness in achieving the goals of global citizenship education: *evaluation*, *appraisal*, and *assessment*. Institutional evaluation is the cocoon within which professional appraisal and student assessment can take place. All are interrelated and essential components of the effective delivery of global citizenship education, but they serve different functions. In the first case, evaluation is a macro appraisal of the appropriateness and effectiveness of the institutional and instructional achievement of the school's overall goals. It is inevitably an engagement with means and ends, with the values and ethos of the institution and its overall mission, and includes a review of the institution as a whole, its policies and curricula, as well as the performance of its staff and the attainment of its students.

Appraisal is the review of the professional effectiveness of the staff of the school. It may comprise self-appraisal, dyadic intervisiting, group approaches, institutional discourse and formal professional appraisal. Its focus is predominantly on the extent to which the teacher is adhering to the overall mission of the school for students, and on the professional development necessary to make that achievement more 'perfect'. It is often seen as threatening and problematic by teachers. There is an absence of good objective measures on the basis of which professional judgements may be made, and we still await the further development of professional evaluation techniques which evaluate teachers' thinking and decision-making skills as well as their classroom behaviours and knowledge.[25]

Assessment is the appraisal of the learning gains of the students, through the monitoring of their performance on cognitive, affective and behavioural indicators. The main aim of assessment is to ensure that each student's attainment can be helpfully and clearly identified, as part of the process of identifying strengths and weaknesses, in such a way that the results can be used to facilitate and support the student's further progress.

OVERALL POLICY GOALS FOR EVALUATION, APPRAISAL AND ASSESSMENT

As a first step, therefore, to the construction and implementation of an effective strategy for assessment and evaluation of global citizenship education, one must set down a framework policy for evaluation, appraisal and assessment within the school. Such a strategy is part of but critically interactive with the overall mission statement for the school, which expresses and, to the extent possible in human affairs and the current stage of our expertise, focuses on teachers' professional judgement of students and teachers' reflective appraisal of themselves and their institution. The issues include:

(a) the ways in which the school seeks to foster the development of qualities of empathy with other human beings, a sensitivity to human diversity and similarity, dependence and interdependence;

(b) how the school aims to enhance the social literacy of staff and students, including their intercultural competence to relate creatively to the diversity of human cultures;

(c) whether students on leaving school have a greater awareness of the causes of human conflicts at the interpersonal, intergroup and international levels, and have developed the ability and commitment to engage for their creative and just resolution;

(d) whether the students are committed to combating prejudice, discrimination and social injustice, wherever they arise;

(e) how far and in what ways the school community cherishes an appreciation of the worthy achievements of all individuals and human groups, and an ambition to build on and extend them;

(f) how successfully members of the school community demonstrate the internalization of agreed, reflective moral bases for human behaviour in culturally diverse communities, societies and international contexts;

(g) in what ways members of the school develop an understanding of human–ecosystem interdependence and of individual, group and national responsibility for creative and accountable environmental custodianship;

(h) how far there is awareness of human economic interdependence and of the need for responsible pursuit of economic satisfaction;

(i) in what ways students develop the skills necessary for them to take up responsible roles as individual, family member, citizen, worker and consumer within democratic, culturally diverse human societies;

(j) whether they manifest qualities of imagination, inquisitiveness and rationality and are committed to applying these to responsible cultural, social, economic and environmental activity.[26]

INSTITUTIONAL AND INSTRUCTIONAL EVALUATION

Any institutional evaluation needs to bear in mind that the culture (and subcultures) of the institution may influence not only what is taught, but how it is taught, when it is taught and how successfully. Thus an evaluation of the contextual quality of the school must include items addressing its culture and values. Beyond the more general characteristics, the mechanics for the just implementation and assessment of global citizenship education need to address how far the school is successful in providing:

(a)   an ordered 'respect for persons' environment, which is conducive to the learning and social development of children, which sets high expectations for the behaviour and work of all members of the school community and which engenders a commitment to human rights, excellence, justice and equality;

(b)   an ethos of trustworthiness, mutuality and human reciprocity in all members of the school community, so that staff and students demonstrate respect and concern for others, their opinions and values and an ability to engage in discourse to overcome conflict and to resolve human contradictions and dilemmas;

(c)   a structure where the intellectual, emotional, physical, spiritual and moral development of students is developed to their full potential;

(d)   a diversity of media for the appreciation (and expression of appreciation) of human achievements and excellence in all fields and a desire to achieve similar standards;

(e)   enhancement of the self-esteem, self-confidence and social responsibility of pupils and staff;

(f)   a school organization committed to human rights secured within the rule of law and the practice of pluralist democracy;

(g)   understanding and expression of the interdependence of humans with their ecosystem, through the involvement of pupils in local measures for environmental conservation;

(h)   an ambience of economic literacy and responsibility, emphasizing the interdependence of economic and environmental decisions and of communities and nations;

(i)   preparation for active citizenship in their communities, their nation and the world and development of the appropriate skills and expertise;

(j)   a concern for the school and wider environment which is carefully nurtured as part of the school's culture.

Such goals may not be susceptible to exact calibration as part of the overall evaluation process or to precise statistical measurement in the way that cognitive learning gains may be, but they are there to be perceived and they can be excellent fare for a mixed-method, dialogical evaluation of an institutional and instructional commitment to global citizenship education. Such a mixed-method methodology may serve many purposes at all stages of the evaluation process.[27]

Of course, such a process for evaluating an institution assumes that there are at least provisional criteria for judging programmes in citizenship education and, in turn, that there are well articulated objectives against which the effective delivery of the programme can be reviewed, which are themselves subject to review. Here, we are helped by some of the work, defining citizenship expertise, designed in the 1970s, including the identification of what are called by Remy seven basic citizenship competences:

(a)   in the acquisition and processing of information about political situations;

(b) in the assessment of one's own involvement and stake in political situations, issues, decisions and policies;

(c) in thoughtful decision-making regarding group governance and problems of citizenship;

(d) in developing and using standards, such as justice, ethics, morality, and practicality, to make judgements of people, institutions, policies and decisions;

(e) in the communication of ideas to other citizens, decision-makers, leaders and officials;

(f) in cooperating and working with others in groups and organizations to achieve mutual goals; and

(g) in working with bureaucratically organized institutions in order to promote and protect one's interests and values.[28]

These seven 'areas of competence' are incomplete for our purposes in this book, and there are clearly 'missing' dimensions from the totality of global citizenship education. These missing dimensions would include the recognition of three interactive, perhaps even symbiotic, levels of citizenship, international interdependence across the domains of knowledge and the environmental dimension. But, as far as they go, the 'competences' are certainly not incompatible with 'our' concept of citizenship. Moreover, carrying the discussion of the purposes of citizenship education forward into its evaluation, Remy makes three suggestions which are in accord with the concept of citizenship education being advanced in this book: that citizenship curricula should be broad, realistic and practical; that they should reflect global interdependence; and that they should express the diversity of society. On that basis, he suggests a number of criteria for judging citizenship programmes, such as:

(a) the breadth of the concept of citizenship on which the curriculum is based;

(b) the extent of coverage of the competences needed by citizens to discharge their duties and responsibilities as citizens and to protect their interests;

(c) how far the curriculum conveys, not only the ideals of democracy, but also the realities of political life;

(d) the incorporation by the curriculum of information about the practicalities of politics and their process, as well as information about government and legal institutions and structures;

(e) the extent to which the curriculum reflects the diversity of society;

(f) how far the curriculum reflects a global concept of citizenship;

(g) the soundness of the instructional design of the curriculum.[29]

Consequent on such efforts, the National Council for the Social Studies formulated a set of criteria in the form of a checklist of the essential characteristics of a citizenship education programme.[30] Those criteria include items such as clarity, sequencing, integration with the rest of the curriculum; relevance, scope, including local, national and international dimensions; global focus, participatory, activity and experiential nature; the way in which it affords the development of a balanced approach to rights and responsibilities at the various levels of community appurtenance; the extent to which it develops students' competence to make decisions in a perspicacious manner; its success in generating standards of justice, ethics, morality and practicality to make logical and fair judgements; and its inbuilt capacity for comprehensive and continuous evaluation.

Some practical evaluations of citizenship education programmes have provided opportunities for the development of improvement-oriented research, where the main objective is to achieve better professional practice and learning outcomes in schools.[31] One such project was the ICE Project (Improving Citizenship Education) in Atlanta, Georgia in the early 1980s. It addressed five questions of process evaluation and two of product evaluation, which are helpful to our purposes in raising some of the issues about institutional evaluation in this chapter. The process evaluation questions focused on:

(a)   how much the teachers learned about teaching procedures in the staff development sessions;

(b)   how supportive the teachers considered their administrators to be during implementation of the citizenship project;

(c)   how useful teachers found the delineated objectives of the project;

(d)   how helpful the teachers found the community resources identified for the project; and

(e)   how helpful the teachers found the curriculum materials provided or developed under the project.

In addition to the above five process evaluation issues, there were two product evaluation questions, concerning;

(a)   whether there was significant and practical difference between the political knowledge of project and control students; and

(b)   whether there was a significant and practical difference between the political attitudes of project and control students.[32]

A number of matters are worthy of attention in the above suggested evaluation questions. Firstly, they do not comprehend a holistic institutional evaluation, nor do they recognize any institutional 'case law' of evaluation, if it exists. Secondly, there is little evidence of the dialogical institutional and professional process, which is a *sine qua non* for global citizenship education. Thirdly, they are really concerned in the product section with the assessment of students. Fourthly, they are not focused on the evaluation of improvements in the professional practice of teachers in their classroom teaching. Fifthly, they do not contain any reference to behaviour in the product domain. For global citizenship education, it would be essential to develop a process which could also address the above issues, within the context of a holistic institutional, curricular, professional and students' evaluation, reflective of human rights and social responsibilities.

Yet the ICE Project theorized that the provision of five major areas of support to teachers would result in changes in the classroom activities and content of teachers and through that the citizenship attitudes and knowledge of students. As our purpose here is not to evaluate either the project and its effectiveness in reaching its espoused objectives or the validity of its evaluation, but rather to learn from it what we can for the development of our own strategy of evaluation for global citizenship education, it should be noted that it was focused on curriculum improvement. The strategy for curriculum improvement is directly relevant to the evaluation of global citizenship education, combining five major factors:

(a) delineation of curriculum goals and objectives;
(b) staff development to enhance teaching skills considered necessary for citizenship education;
(c) identification or development of needed curriculum materials;
(d) identification of and access to useful community resources; and
(e) administrative support.[33]

Again, while such 'support' is an essential part of the delivery of citizenship education (and its evaluation), it is probably insufficient to deliver two major dimensions of global citizenship education. The first is the creation of a more open classroom climate, where students can participate in decision-making and are encouraged to raise and challenge views and positions in both subject-matter and peer and teacher presentations, as a means to cognitive and effective moral growth. The second also relates directly to the classroom and concerns the developmentally fruitful use of controversy, so as to generate respect for others, their views and cultures and the introduction of collaborative ways of working, based on the values of mutuality and reciprocity.[34]

These two characteristics are major dimensions of global citizenship education and it is important to understand why they are a core and integral part rather than just an optional or peripheral characteristic. For global citizenship education, it is essential that students are prepared for the hurly-burly of the real world, nation and communities, where all is not sweetness and light, harmony and unanimity. So, it is important that students are prepared for sensitivity to conflict, and have the ability to make conflict creative and to understand and analyse moral dilemmas of good–good and good–bad kinds. Unless schools and their curricula can prepare students for this process at the three typical levels of citizenship and across all the domains of knowledge, students will be ill-prepared for active citizenship in pluralist democracies.

Schools must not consider evaluation of their citizenship education as merely a matter of evaluation of their programmes. Schools can control more than their programmes; they must realize that they are, in a real sense, political systems, where there must be a high level of congruence between declared and operative values, between talking about the virtue of democratic participation and delivering it in the very fabric of their every-day lives.[35] Thus, these elements need to be embraced in both the institutional and instructional evaluation processes for global citizenship education, sensitive to human diversity, attentive to its political and cultural pluralism, congruent with human rights and social responsibilities, conscious of its environmental dimensions and based on respect for persons and equal social justice, all aimed at cognitive, affective and conative attainments.

So to return to the combination of these two elements, any evaluation, appraisal or assessment of the achievement by the school and its members of its global citizenship objectives needs to take into account the institutional context and the extent to which that context influences the achievement of learning goals. As argued earlier, that context comprises both *organizational* and *processual* characteristics (as proposed in Chapter 4; see pp. 70–71) which together would represent the school and instructional parameters, within which effective global citizenship education could be delivered. The following questions must be posed about those two sets of characteristics:

Organizational

(a)   Is there a strong institutional leadership committed to the principles of human rights and democratic participation in the delivery of global citizenship education?

(b)   Is there an explicit emphasis on global citizenship education in curriculum, instruction and assessment, including both content and procedures?

(c)   Are the educational and narrower instructional goals of the school articulated in the form of a clear institutional and instructional statement, addressing issues of citizenship, which is subject to effective communication and discussion with parents, teachers and students?

(d)   Are there uniformly high academic, behavioural and participatory expectations for both staff and students, based on respect for persons, mutuality, reciprocity and due process?

(e)   Does the school acknowledge and reward both academic and worthwhile non-academic achievements?

(f)   Are there humane and interactive evaluation and monitoring procedures, which are effective yet attentive to human integrity and sensitivity; and do they include the evaluation of the performance of all members of the school community?

(g)   Is there a developmental perspective on the continuing professional evolution of staff in global citizenship education, including human rights and law-related aspects?

(h)   Is there meaningful involvement and support of parents and the community?

(i)   What measures have been introduced to involve members of the school community in environmental preservation and development?

(j)   How does the school deal with recalcitrants and delinquent behaviour? Are there express procedures for appeal, negotiation and mediation?

(k)   How does the school deal with those children who have special educational needs?

(l)   How does the school create opportunities for students of all ages to undertake responsible school 'citizenship'?

Traditional educational evaluations tend, as Fraser has argued, to neglect process criteria, partly because these latter are less concrete.[36] Yet, in global citizenship education, the school and classroom environments are crucial to the learning of values of cooperation, mutual trust and ethical reciprocity and to the creative incumbency of responsible positions in school and classroom. It would therefore be important that any overall evaluation strategy should include process as well as achievement criteria. These might include:

Process

(a)   In what ways has a system of strategic values and assumptions directed to human rights, social responsibility and global citizenship been built up?

(b)   Is there an effective level of verbal and oral communication between all parties, based on the principle of respect for persons?

(c)   Are there explicit and well-promulgated procedures for collaborative planning and implementation of changes?

(d)   Does the school endorse democracy in the classroom in the form of participatory methods of learning, commitment to cooperative methods and social activities in school and community?

(e)   How convincingly is the school's ethos committed to human rights and democracy and in what ways could it be improved?

(f)   Is the principle of equal justice manifestly a core value of the school?

(g)   Is there an explicit commitment to due process for all?

(h)   Is there close attentiveness and congruence with children's stage of development and interests?

Such questions need to be refined and made participatory, before they can be utilized for evaluation, yet they are crucially contextual to the five indispensable elements of global citizenship education at the classroom level: ethical and moral education; critical and reflexive thinking; knowledge and expertise of the democratic process; developmental approaches; and commitment to human rights and social responsibilities (see pp. 56–61). These five elements were regarded and advocated as indispensable to the achievement of the overall goals of education in culturally diverse societies, as to the more specific attainment of the goals of citizenship education within that context.

PROFESSIONAL APPRAISAL

As stated above, the issue of professional evaluation has a brief but fraught history. At a time when the ideologies of greater accountability and value for money hold sway in both developed and developing countries, there is a marked decline in the status of teachers, and increasingly teachers are demoted to the technicist role of cultural non-commissioned officers. There is a tendency to overemphasize external control, quantifiable cognitive outcomes and system conformity. As part of that movement, a number of states in the United States have inaugurated more extensive regimens of teacher evaluation, including observational systems, which have a tendency to over-simplify complex cultural situations. Sometimes the standards for such evaluation, while resting on an overall conceptual framework related to the field, are seen as the property of evaluators rather than jointly agreed with the professionals who are being evaluated.[37]

The emphasis solely on external approaches, which do not endorse the reflective dimensions of a teacher's work, could be short-sighted and misguided; the greater the onus that can be placed on teachers themselves to call their own professional practice to the bar of an accountability whose criteria they share, the greater the real chance of quality improvement.[38] There is evidence that teachers rate more highly a system of evaluation which will facilitate their professional growth, individually and collegially, by encouraging them to reflect on their practice.[39] In any case the appraisal of teachers, whether self-appraisal or institutional, has to be responsive to the overall principles of evaluation for global citizenship, based on human rights and freedoms. It will need to manifest respect for persons, a commitment to due process, to mutuality and reciprocity and to human justice.

Reflective professionals, who are attempting to deliver global citizenship education, must ask themselves certain questions, and these questions arise from the nature of the exercise. They relate to and are at the same time expressive of the values and basic ethic of the professional practice of teaching about, according to and for human rights. They would surely include:

(a)   What methods do I adopt to monitor my own teaching and what means do I have for scrutinizing my objectives?

(b)   How successful am I in motivating my students to adopt values and behaviour which are expressive of human rights and social responsibilities?

(c)   How systematic and coherent am I in reinforcing values and behaviour which are conducive to global citizenship education?

(d)   How good am I at constructing situations in which my students can demonstrate their learning in the form of behaviour? How can I improve?

(e)   How 'democratic' is my classroom environment? How can its 'democracy' be improved?

(f)   How far is my professional practice in all its aspects consistent with the principle of respect for persons?

(g)   In what ways do I make my teaching, content and methods expressive of the three levels of citizenship described in this book?

(h)   Are my professional judgements conducive to due process and free from social and cultural bias?

(i)   Do I make efforts to engage students actively in their own learning?

(j)   How successful am I in communicating a commitment to mutuality and reciprocity to fellow professionals and to students?

(k)   Are there unexploited opportunities in my syllabus for issues of human rights or law-related issues to be introduced?

(l)   How global is the perspective I adopt to issues of economics and the environment?

(m)   How far am I acquainted with the diversity of cultures among my students, and how comfortable do I feel with it?

(n)   Can I improve the ways in which I find out about the extent to which I achieve my teaching/learning objectives?

ASSESSING THE ACHIEVEMENT OF LEARNING OBJECTIVES

There are basically two modes of student assessment recognized in the contemporary literature: competitive and non-competitive. Both forms of assessment may be used to monitor the progress of students in achieving the knowledge, skills and insights of global citizenship education. Given that neither is wholly incompatible with its goals and basic ethic, the task for the skilful educator is to find a blend of both forms of assessment, which will facilitate those methods and approaches which are best able to deliver global citizenship education. Thus, insofar as cooperative ways of working are to be fostered, non-competitive forms of assessment are best suited, while for the assessment of cognitive knowledge, competitive modes may well be more applicable to provide incentives.[40] Moreover, both may contribute to a longitudinal record of achievement, which can comprehend those dimensions of human learning and non-academic performance which are often so neglected in the overall profile of human development, but which are central to the morality of judgement and behaviour at the core of global citizenship education.[41] We need to bear in mind the impact of the medium chosen for assessment on the learning of the students, and the values they acquire informally from the message contained in the chosen mode of assessment.

The assessment of educational achievement usually concentrates on the skills, understandings and knowledge which students acquire as a result of their participation in educational programmes. Tests may be either norm-referenced, where norms are constructed on the basis of students' results in the tests, or criterion-referenced, where a level of knowledge or a particular score on a bank of items is predetermined by the teacher or some other agency. These two approaches are not mutually exclusive and are often used interactively. Sometimes both the definition and the strategy adopted may include values and attitudes, as well as cognitive knowledge. In the case of citizenship education, standardized tests have been constructed to attempt to review student achievement across a range of indicators, and these can be more broadly based rather than concentrated on one aspect of citizenship education, such as law-related education.[42] Sometimes the strategies include both process and product indicators, related to staff and students.[43] In none of these cases is the accuracy of the existing tests on a par with the accuracy of instruments for the measurement of weight, distance, volume or temperature in the natural sciences.

At the core of global citizenship education are the objectives of enabling students to achieve quite specific *understandings*, *attitudes* and *skills and behaviours*, which derive from its basic values and the epistemology that derives from those values. But while it is relatively easy to list such objectives, they represent a particular challenge to the educator, assessor and evaluator, not least because of the lack of maturity of the field and the lack of overall consensus about what good citizenship entails and how it can best be demonstrated, and that in spite of substantial progress in the United States in the early 1980s.[44] A recent survey of the extent to which states in the United States have promoted what is a major dimension of global citizenship education, teaching for understanding and thinking in elementary schools, found that only very few had any kind of coherent policy to encourage teaching for higher-level attainments.[45] Only one state, California, was found to have curriculum frameworks which described the philosophy and nature of instructional programmes in each content area and which were backed up by a detailed assessment programme stressing higher-order thinking and communicating a consistent message for increased emphasis on understanding and thinking.

And yet assessing for cognitive attainment in terms of facts, principles, concepts and generalizations is fairly straightforward. There are existing precedents and instruments and there may be sound reasons for using existing test instruments in the social sciences. But when one comes to assess complex conceptual knowledge, process skills, and higher-order thinking, the process becomes much more complex, open-ended, less charted and more difficult.[46] Even more, the appraisal of social skills, such as democratic participation, critical thinking and research skills, may be susceptible to monitoring through the use of standardized instruments, but are the tests testing what is intended or are they a surrogate for the real thing? With values and attitudes, appraisal presents an even bleaker picture, with numerous theoretical works and very little practical progress.

Even if personal interviews are utilized to assess values and attitudes, the problems of standardization and availability loom large for the average class teacher, and there is still the problem of a longitudinal perspective on achievements across cognitive, affective and behavioural domains.

One possibility is to use tests for the cognitive aspects of global citizenship education, and to adopt profiles as a more broadly conceived but finely calibrated approach to longitudinal records of achievement.[47] Such a profile could record the assessment of skills besides the traditional subject-matter, communicative competence orally and written, responsibilities undertaken, personal qualities, such as initiative, ability to work cooperatively in groups, perseverance and self-image, as well as other non-academic outcomes. It could also include items of student self-assessment, self-analysis and description, all of which could be continually updated. Such a combined approach might be better able to embrace the learning outcomes for students identified in Chapter 2. Certainly any meaningful evaluation would need to address answers to the issue of how far the programme had been successful in delivering the following understandings:

(a)   of the similarities and differences of human beings, their values, locations and styles of social and political life and the influence of these on individuals, groups, societies and the world community;

(b)   of economic and environmental interdependence at local, national and international levels;

(c)   of the varying ways in which pluralist democracies work;

(d)   of the major human rights and responsibilities at the three levels and in social, cultural, economic and environmental spheres;

(e)   of the varying ways in which legal systems in pluralist democracies function.

Such a profile approach would also need to address the issue of values and attitudes and the assessment of affective objectives, which could be done by either observational approaches or by asking closed response or more unstructured questions. Approaches such as essays, simulations and role-playing by the students are confounded by the fact that often the goals are not clear, by the fact that the values and attitudes depend on the developmental stage of the children, and finally by the lack of reliability of observational judgements. Moreover, at least three separable but overlapping domains of values and attitudes may be discerned in the literature: those pertaining to social values, those which address intellectual values, and those which specifically address citizenship attitudes and values.

The field is further complicated by the fact that so many of these attitudes and values are not exclusive to citizenship education, but may be shared with other domains of the curriculum or part of the whole school strategy. Not only do we lack specific instruments and precedents which would assist in more refined assessment of student progress, but the usual vicarious approach to assessing commitment, by asking students how they would act or feel, is not ideal and may be subject to both distortion and fundamental change over time. A stated commitment may only reflect what the student perceives that he or she is expected to say.

What is really needed is a combined evaluation and assessment approach which can address the main component parts of global citizenship education, not solely in terms of cognitive achievement but especially in terms of values, attitudes and skills. Those objectives of evaluation will be concerned with the provision of opportunities for students to demonstrate learning of values and attitudes, skills and expertise such as:

(a)   the extent to which students have developed, can state and demonstrate a commitment to the values of human rights, social justice and pluralist democracy;

(b)   how far students, consistent with their developmental stage, can express reciprocity, empathy and mutuality in all human affairs, whether cultural, social, economic, political or environmental;

(c)   the ways in which students are able to demonstrate a willingness to participate in civic life at appropriate levels;

(d)   the extent to which students feel comfortable with cultural diversity, by demonstrating attitudes of openness to the cultures and ideas of others and mutuality in human relations;

(e)   the ways in which students manifest a strong commitment to gender and racial equality and willingness to engage socially and politically for them;

(f)   the willingness of the student to engage in persuasion and dialogue as the major means to achieve social justice and change;

(g)   students' awareness of gender, cultural and national stereotyping and bias in their own culture and language and engagement to overcome them;

(h)   autonomous but socially responsible moral judgement and integrity, based on reflective and clarified values;

(i)   acceptance of the provisionality of human social and moral knowledge and the uncertainty which this implies;

(j)   responsible consumer and producer skills, responsive to the human and environmental rights of others;

(k)   engagement for human rights, justice and dignity;

(l)   ability to evaluate the economic, social, political and environmental decisions of others objectively;

(m)   interpersonal competence and the ability to make and maintain good human relationships in different cultural contexts and across professional, personal and civic domains;

(n)   ability to dialogue and discourse within and across cultures;

(o)   communicative competence across a range of media and registers of language;

(p)   political literacy including the capacity for creative dissent, problem-solving, advocacy and creative conflict resolution;

(q)   decision-making, participatory and collaborative competencies;

All of the above learning outcomes for students have to be seen within the holistic context of four overlapping elements: institutional and programme evaluation, staff professional appraisal and student assessment. Each layer is an interactive part of the system as a whole. It is quite possible, for example, for poor policies and practices at the school level to be inimical to the effective achievement of objectives at the instructional level and vice versa. Therefore any evaluation for global citizenship education has to skilfully design component parts of the evaluation which can address the four elements above without destroying the coherence and unity of the whole process. In this process, however, we are helped by the fact that the very process of evaluation in its four elements and as a whole can be a further means to the achievement of the goals of global citizenship education. The process of consultation, involvement and participation as part of evaluation in a structural and ethical context which recognizes diversity, democracy and respect for persons is not solely evaluation, it is also the practice of global citizenship education.

RESOURCES FOR DEVELOPMENT AND EVALUATION

There is a sense in which the chapters of this book have already indicated the kinds of resources available to educators and others in their search for guidance and information in introducing and evaluating global citizenship education into their school and into their teaching. They have also indicated the kind of training which will be necessary for school staffs as a whole and for individual educators. Each chapter is supported by notes, documenting the progress of the argument and assisting the reader to validate and evaluate its case. Moreover, at the conclusion of this volume there is also an extensive list of books and articles for further reading, being sources not quoted in the notes but none the less interesting and informative on the subject of global citizenship education.

The aim of this section, therefore, is to provide a brief synoptic overview of the various resource domains available for introducing global citizenship; an outline sketch rather than a detailed map. It is intended to be indicative and exemplary rather than exhaustive and to draw on sources which may be readily available to educators and schools. Its concern is two-fold: human resource development and the acquisition of material resources.

BIBLIOGRAPHIC SOURCES AND SEARCHES

There are numerous resources available to the educator to introduce the approach to citizenship education advocated in this book. Educators' needs are not, however, all the same. Thus, as part of institutional evaluation and professional appraisal, there must be an assessment of needs. Schools work in different cultural, legal, ideological and regulatory contexts and those, as well as institutional ethos and history, curriculum fit, teacher interest and competence, have to be taken into account in the selection, evaluation and acquisition of material for teaching.

One of the easiest and most immediate ways of gaining an overview of the literature is by undertaking a computerized bibliographic search. The most extensive database of material for the field described by this book would be available through the ERIC system. Other databases such as EUDISEC, Education Index, British Education Index, the Canadian Education Index, the Australian Education Index and the International Index of Bibliography on Education may also be useful, although they possess large amounts of non-English-language material which may be of limited use. The systems mentioned have different descriptors, but all would yield relevant material through descriptors such as citizenship education, civics, civic education or more broadly political education. Moreover, subtopics on which any curriculum for global citizenship education must draw may also be searched. These might include law-related education, although that term is still problematic, insofar as it yields a lot of material about education for legal and paralegal professions; it therefore needs to be combined with other terms to refine the search. Further terms associated with cognate areas will include environmental education or studies, peace education, global studies, social studies, multicultural and intercultural education, values education, principle-testing, global approaches, science and technology in society (STS), ecological education, development education, democracy and democratic principles, consumer education, current events, games and simulation, world studies. There will also be cross-themes, such as school effectiveness, curriculum development, school organization, participation, evaluation and assessment, discrimination and prejudice, and developing countries.

A search which covered all of these descriptors, however, would be too large for most educators' needs and would probably be too unwieldy to be of use to teachers in schools, especially if they included both book and non-book materials. Moreover, some of the non-book material is rapidly overtaken, as it is initially submitted in the form of papers presented to conferences, which are later revised and published in journals or as chapters in symposia. Thus one must focus more closely on the aspect of citizenship education which is under investigation. Any of the descriptors above would probably have considerable overlap with the others, so one or two of them could be combined with delimiters such as the dates within which the search is to be conducted and the level of education, namely primary and secondary education.

Such areas can be made more manageable and relevant by combining them with the elements of the conceptualization introduced in Chapter 3. The five major elements which were defined as being indispensable to global citizenship education in that chapter and which were used in subsequent chapters were: ethical and moral education; critical and reflexive thinking; knowledge and expertise of the democratic process; developmental approaches; and commitment to human rights and social responsibilities. These elements were seen as being attentive to the three typical levels of citizenship and the domains of focus introduced in the earlier chapters, and the principles of procedure defined for the book in the Introduction. Each of these five areas combined with the descriptors above would yield a substantial amount of material in the ERIC system. The material would probably contain speculative and theoretical papers, both published and unpublished, reports of empirical investigations, curriculum development and evaluation, reports of classroom practice, as well as more substantial textbook materials. It is important too to note that there is a fairly extensive dissertation section to the ERIC database, which can also be searched, and some of this material is imaginative, insightful and unique, in both content and methodology.

Attention should also be given to the various abstracting services, such as Psychological or Sociological Abstracts, which can provide up-to-date information on a similar key-word basis, and to the international journals and periodicals which may cover the field or subfields. Handbooks, yearbooks, dictionaries, guides to educational information, both published and local, and encyclopedias of education may also yield either 'leads' or directly useful information. There is too a wide spread of both national and international journals and periodicals, many of which have been referred to in this book, which can provide useful theoretical insights, or even on occasions practical tips and guidance. In this latter category comes the series known as Updates in Law-related Education.

NATIONAL AND INTERNATIONAL ORGANIZATIONS

Many international organizations produce materials, reports, commentaries, statistical data, yearbooks, classroom aids and books for teaching and library purposes, which can be of use in adopting a more global and community-sensitive approach to citizenship education. The best sources for human rights materials are either the United Nations (particularly the Centre for Human Rights) in New York, the Council of Europe in Strasbourg or voluntary organizations such as Amnesty International or the British-based Minority Rights Group. United Nations agencies such as UNICEF produce year-books on the state of the world's children, as well as materials on children's rights, the World Bank produces an annual World Development Report (1990 was concerned with world poverty), as well as materials for classroom use, and UNESCO has a long tradition of the production of materials in the area of environmental education, all of which were useful in the production of this book. Oxfam, Action-Aid, the Council for Education in World Citizenship, the British Commission for Racial Equality, the Commonwealth Institute, Runnymede Trust, and the Anti-Defamation League (which has offices in many countries), all produce materials which with appropriate professional scrutiny can be used in schools. Civil Rights or Human Rights Commissions in countries such as the United States and Canada are also invaluable sources of information and ideas.

There is also now a network of offices for law-related education in each state in the United States, including a National Institute for Citizen Education in the Law, and a new Citizenship Foundation was recently established in London. In the United States, the Council for the Advancement of Citizenship and the Center for Civic Education have recently concluded collaboration in a major new framework for civic education, entitled CIVITAS. The American Federation of Teachers (of which John Dewey was a founder member), the Educational Excellence Network and Freedom House have combined in a joint project on education for democracy and are assisting in the development of materials and structures being utilized in Eastern Europe and some Latin American countries. The Council for the Advancement of Citizenship also produces numerous publications and a newsletter. The Children's Legal Centre in London both produces and distributes very useful factsheets on the rights of children, and these are useful for teaching about children's rights. Several of the above organizations produce catalogues which contain teaching materials and other educational texts in the field covered by this book.

TRAINING AND PREPARING

Throughout this book, I have emphasized the radical but evolutionary nature of a professional commitment to global citizenship education. In previous chapters, I indicated the way in which it could grow from the ethos and values of 'good' teachers and effective schools. The more the process of training can rest on the individual institution's evaluation of its own needs and its staff's perception of needed change the easier will be the task of introducing global citizenship education which is attentive to human rights and expressive of social responsibilities.

Certainly, there are many academic institutions where global courses or courses on human rights, even on citizenship, may be attended on a part- or full-time basis. There are even networks in some cases, to give support and information to educators. But such strategies can never be complete in themselves and they need to be amplified by the collegial efforts of staff and the commitment of individual professionals. For that reason, the path of staff discourse has to be the one first trodden. It is the reality constructed by individual teachers and students, in the daily lives of their schools and classrooms, which will do more to construct a human rights sensitive global citizenship education, than the provision of formal courses.

PROFESSIONAL VALIDATION

As in the previous chapters, this chapter concludes with a section of dialogue, in which the reader is invited to take critical distance from the writer and the text. In a sense, this process is more important in this chapter because it is the final chapter of the book, and what is needed is a reflection on the book as a whole as well as on the content and proposals made in this chapter. In that context, it seems appropriate firstly to raise issues of evaluation as described and analysed in this chapter, before then proceeding to an overall reflection on the book as a whole.

In the context of the points made about evaluation in this chapter, it may be important to raise questions such as:

(a)　What is the institutional biography and tradition of evaluation? Are there pre-existing case laws of evaluation? What kinds of staff skills exist for the mounting of evaluations?

(b)　Does the school have a mission statement, and, if so, is it regularly updated? What is the process of review? How participatory is it? Who is involved and why?

(c)　Is there a pre-existing system of staff appraisal? How relevant were the criticisms of some systems of staff appraisal contained in this chapter to your own context? Are there opportunities for intervisiting by staff, for peer-pairing for evaluation, for institutional linking and mutual assistance?

(d)　How are the current curricula decided and evaluated? Are there external as well as internal agencies involved? Do the criteria conform to the criteria enunciated in this book for global citizenship education? In what ways would you like to see them changed and why?

(e)　What are the current procedures for student assessment and for the recording and communication of that assessment? Do the strategies and instruments address non-cognitive attainments? How are non-academic achievements recognized in the institutional values system?

At the level of the book as a whole, it is important to cast a valedictory reflection on the propositions advanced in it and the case for a more global and differentiated concept of citizenship education as an element in the school life of every school. The reader may wish to ask a number of questions, including;

(a)　Am I convinced by the case put forward in this book for global citizenship education?

(b) How clear is the concept of global citizenship education and in what ways does it need to be changed?

(c) How far do I share the values and assumptions contained in this book about human nature and human rights and justice?

(d) How practical is it to expect such ideals and values to be incorporated in the schooling of children in my institution and system?

(e) How clear are the strategies for the development of global citizenship in this book?

(f) What elements can I use in the improvement of my own professional practice and that of my colleagues and school?

(g) What changes would I make in the material of the book, or what additions would I like to see made?

(h) Against what criteria can I evaluate this book and the case for global citizenship education which it has advanced? How far are they already implicit within it, or how far do I need to generate them myself?

(i) If I consider the case at least partially valid and its continuation worthwhile, in what ways can I continue and advance the dialogue initiated by this book between writer and reader to a wider circle of professional and lay personnel?

(j) What professional responsibility do I share and recognize for the advancement of a citizenship education for all children, which embraces some or all the characteristics advanced in this volume for global citizenship education and how can I fulfil that responsibility?

NOTES AND REFERENCES

1. Carnegie Forum on Education and the Economy (1986) *A Nation Prepared: Teachers for the 21st Century* (New York: Carnegie Corporation).

2. The distinction between analysis and evaluation is well elucidated by Ariav, T. (1986) 'Curriculum analysis and curriculum evaluation: a contrast', *Studies in Educational Evaluation*, 12, 139–47.

3. Peterson, P. L. and Comeaux, M. A. (1990) 'Evaluating the systems: teachers' perspectives on teacher evaluation', *Educational Analysis and Policy Analysis*, 12(1), 3–24.

4. See Nowakowski, J. (1990) 'Exploring the role of professional standards in evaluations: areas of needed research', *Studies in Educational Evaluation*, 16, 271–96.

5. Scriven, M. (1967) *The Methodology of Evaluation*. AERA Monograph Series in Curriculum Evaluation No. 1. (Chicago, IL: Rand McNally). For a coherent overview of mixed-method approaches, see Greene, J. C., Caracelli, V. J. and Graham, W. F. (1989) 'Toward a conceptual framework for mixed-method evaluation designs', *Educational Evaluation and Policy Analysis*, 11(3), 255–74.

6. An interesting analysis of the impediments in one project is Ziegahn, L. (1989) 'Internal evaluation in a developing organization: impediments to implementation', *Studies in Educational Evaluation*, 15, 163–81.

7. A useful overview of tools for school self-evaluation is provided in McKenzie, P. A. and Harrold, R. (1990) 'Tools for school self-evaluation: developments in Australia', *Studies in Educational Evaluation*, 15, 31–45.

8. McLaughlin, M. W. and Pfeifer, R. S. (1988) *Teacher Evaluation: Improvement, Accountability, and Effective Learning* (New York: Teachers' College Press).

9. See, in this connection, Lieberman, A. (ed.) (1988) *Building a Professional Culture in Schools* (New York: Teachers' College Press).

10. Sparks, G. (1988) 'Teacher attitudes towards change and subsequent improvements in

classroom teaching', *Journal of Educational Psychology*, **80**, 111–7; and Stein, M. and Wang, M. (1988) 'Teacher development and school improvement: the process of teacher change', *Teaching and Teacher Education*, **4**, 171–87.

11. Rich, Y. (1990) 'Ideological impediments to instructional innovation: the case of cooperative learning', *Teaching and Teacher Education*, **6**(1), 81–91.

12. Fullan, M. (1982) *The Meaning of Educational Change* (New York: Teachers' College Press); and Lieberman, A. and Miller, L. (1984) *Staff Development: New Demands, New Realities and New Perspectives* (New York: Teachers' College Press).

13. One educator who argues that teachers' beliefs flow from their classroom practice and experience and not vice versa is Guskey, T. (1986) 'Staff development and the process of teacher change', *Educational Researcher*, **15**(5), 5–12.

14. See Nisbett, R. and Ross, L. (1980) *Human Inference* (Englewood Cliffs, NJ: Prentice-Hall); and Guskey, T. (1986), 'Staff development and the process of teacher change', *Educational Researcher*, **15**(5), 5–12.

15. MacIntyre, A. (1981) *After Virtue* (Notre Dame, IN: University of Notre Dame Press).

16. Elliott, J. (1990) 'Teachers as researchers: implications for supervision and for teacher education', *Teaching and Teacher Education*, **6**(1), 1–26.

17. Stake, R. E. (1990) 'Situational context as influence on evaluation design and use', *Studies in Educational Evaluation*, **16**, 2321–46.

18. Simons, H. (1987) *Getting to Know Schools in a Democracy: The Politics and Process of Evaluation* (London: Falmer Press).

19. Adelman, C. and Alexander, R. J. (1982) *The Self-Evaluating Institution* (London: Methuen). For a more recent view of the role of the self-evaluating organization in overcoming professional fear or reticence, see Borich, G. D. (1985) 'Needs assessment and the self-evaluating organization', *Studies in Educational Evaluation*, **11**, 205–15.

20. Madaus, G. F. and Stufflebeam, D. (eds) (1989) *Educational Evaluation: The Classic Works of Ralph W. Tyler* (Boston, MA: Kluwer).

21. Some of the questions in this overall section were suggested to me by the Report of the Committee of Enquiry on Discipline in Schools; see Department of Education and Science and Welsh Office (1989) *Discipline in Schools* (London: HMSO).

22. These questions are in part based on Middle States Association of Colleges and Schools (1984) *Handbook for Evaluation Team Members* (Philadelphia, PA: Commission on Higher Education), p. 4.

23. An interesting suggestion which tries to imagine the way which evaluation case histories could be organized by analogy with legal case histories is Caulley, D. N. (1987) 'Evaluation case histories as a parallel to legal case histories: accumulating knowledge and experience in the evaluation profession', *Evaluation and Program Planning*, **10**, 359–72.

24. Weiss, C. (1981) 'Measuring the use of evaluation', in J. Ciarlo (ed.), *Utilizing Evaluation* (Beverly Hills, CA: Sage), pp. 17–29.

25. See, however, Shulman, L. J. and Sykes, G. (1986) 'A National Board for Teaching: in search of a bold new standard', paper prepared for the Task Force on Teaching as a Profession, Carnegie Forum on Education and the Economy (Stanford, CA: Stanford University); and Peterson, P. L. and Comeaux, M. A. (1989) 'Assessing the teacher as a reflective professional: new perspectives on teacher evaluation', in E. Woolfolk (ed.), *The Graduate Preparation of Teachers* (Englewood Cliffs, NJ: Prentice-Hall), pp. 132–52.

26. I have slightly altered the aims, set down in the second chapter, in order to make them more susceptible to absorption into an instrument such as a pro forma or questionnaire for purposes of evaluation.

27. See Greene, J. C., Caracelli, V. J. and Graham, W. F. (1989) 'Toward a conceptual framework for mixed-method evaluation designs', *Educational Evaluation and Policy Analysis*, **11**(3), 255–74.

28. See Remy, R. C. (1980) *Handbook of Basic Citizenship Competences* (Alexandria, VA: Association for Supervision and Curriculum Development).

29. Remy, R. C. (1980) 'Criteria for judging citizenship education programs', *Educational Leadership*, **38**(1), 10–11.

30. National Council for the Social Studies, Citizenship Committee, 1981–3 (1983) 'Essential characteristics of a citizenship education program', *Social Education*, **48**(6), 408–9.
31. For the concept of improvement-oriented research, see Klausmier, H. J. A. (1982) 'A research strategy for educational improvement', *Educational Researcher*, **11**(2), 8–13.
32. Hepburn, M. A. and Napier, J. D. (1984) 'Evaluation of a local improvement-oriented project for citizenship education', *Journal of Educational Research*, **77**(3), 158–65.
33. Napier, J. D. and Grant, E. T. (1986) 'Evaluation of a second generation dissemination of a local improvement project: implications for theory and procedures', *Theory and Research in Social Education*, **14**(1), 67–90.
34. Two pieces of work which endorse the desirability and practicality of including such elements in an overall evaluation strategy are Hawley, W. (1976) *The Implicit Civics Curriculum: Teacher Behavior and Political Learning* (Durham, NC: Duke Center for Policy Analysis); and Ehman, L. (1980) 'The American school in the political socialization process', *Review of Educational Research*, **50**, 99–119.
35. I have found an article by Eyler helpful in the formulation of this section. See Eyler, J. (1980) 'Citizenship education for conflict: an empirical assessment of the relationship between principled thinking and tolerance for conflict and diversity', *Theory and Research in Social Education*, **8**(2), 11–26.
36. Fraser, B. J., Williamson, J. C. and Tobin, K. G. (1987) 'Evaluating alternative high schools in terms of their classroom environments', *Studies in Educational Evaluation*, **12**, 211–17.
37. Joint Committee on Standards for Educational Evaluation (1981) *Standards for Evaluation of Educational Programs, Projects and Materials* (New York: McGraw-Hill).
38. Schon, D. A. (1983) *The Reflective Practitioner: How Professionals Think in Action* (New York: Basic Books).
39. Peterson, P. L. and Comeaux, M. A. (1990) 'Evaluating the systems: teachers' perspectives on teacher evaluation', *Educational Evaluation and Policy Analysis*, **12**(1), 3–24.
40. See Withers, G. and Cornish, G. (1986) 'Non-competitive assessment—its functions and its ideology', *Studies in Educational Evaluation*, **12**, 251–5.
41. Broadfoot, P. (1986) 'Records of achievement: achieving a record?', *Studies in Educational Evaluation*, **12**, 312–23 deals with the different patterns of records, while Withers, G. (1986) 'Profile reports—a typology and some caveats', *Studies in Educational Evaluation*, **12**, 325–34 describes a useful way of conceptualizing a map of the alternative models of profile.
42. See Chambers, B. A. (1982) 'Elementary law-related education program: evaluation report' (Cleveland, OH: Department of Research, Development and Evaluation, Cleveland Public Schools); and DiConstanzo, J. L. (1981) *Review of Selected Standardized Instruments for Use in Citizenship Education* (Pittsburgh, PA: Allegheny Intermediate Unit).
43. Napier, J. D. and Hepburn, M. A. (1982) 'Evaluation of a locally developed social studies curriculum project: improving citizenship education', paper presented at the Annual Meeting of the American Educational Research Association, New York, 1982.
44. Shaver, J. P. (1986) 'National assessment of values and attitudes for social studies', paper prepared for the Study Group on the National Assessment of Student Achievement, and cited as Appendix B in the Final Report, *The Nation's Report Card*.
45. Freeman, D. J. (1989) 'State guidelines promoting teaching for understanding and thinking in elementary schools: a 50-state survey', *Educational Evaluation and Policy Analysis*, **11**(4), 417–29.
46. See Huberman, M. and Cox, P. (1990) 'Evaluation utilization: building links between action and reflection', *Studies in Educational Evaluation*, **16**, 157–79; and King, J. A. (1988) 'Research on evaluation use and its implications for evaluation research and practice', *Studies in Educational Evaluation*, **14**, 285–99.
47. Withers, G. (1986) 'Profile reports: a typology and some caveats', *Studies in Educational Evaluation*, **12**, 325–34.

Further Reading

Action Aid (1988) *GCSE and Standard Grade Project*. London: Action Aid Education Service.

Allport, G.W. (1954) *The Nature of Prejudice*. Reading, MA: Addison-Wesley.

Amir, Y. and Sharan, S. (with the collaboration of Rachel Ben-Ari) (1984) *School Desegregation*. Hilsdale, NJ: Lawrence Erlbaum.

Association for Values Education and Research (1978) *Prejudice*. Toronto: Ontario Institute for Studies in Education.

Association for Values Education and Research (1978) *Prejudice (Teachers Manual)*. Toronto: Ontario Institute for Studies in Education.

Baez, A.V., Knamiller, G.W. and Smyth, J.C. (eds) (1987) *The Environment and Science and Technology Education*. Oxford; Pergamon Press.

Banks, J.A. (1987) *Teaching Strategies for Ethnic Studies*, 4th edn. Boston, MA: Allyn & Bacon.

Banks, J.A. (1988) *Multicultural Education: Theory and Practice*, 2nd edn. Boston, MA: Allyn & Bacon.

Barnes, D. (1976) *From Communication to Curriculum*. Harmondsworth: Penguin.

Beck, C. (1983) *Values and Living*. (Learning Materials for Grades 7 and 8.) Toronto: Ontario Institute for Studies in Education.

Beck, C., McCoy, N. and Bradley-Cameron, J. (1980) *Reflecting on Values*. (Learning Materials for Grades 1–6.) Toronto: Ontario Institute for Studies in Education.

Bernstein, B. (1972) 'On the classification and framing of educational knowledge', in M.F.D. Young (ed.), *Knowledge and Control*. London: Collier-Macmillan.

Boulding, E. (1988) *Building a Global Civic Culture*. New York: Teachers' College, Columbia University.

British Broadcasting Corporation (BBC) (in association with the Secondary Examinations Council) (1987) *Oral English for GCSE and Standard Grade*. London: BBC.

Brown, J. (1983) 'Students' rights', in D. Ray and V. D'Oyley (eds) *Human Rights in Canadian Education*. Dubugue, IA: Kendall/Hunt.

Bruce, J. and Weil, M. (1986) *Models of Teaching*. Englewood Cliffs, NJ: Prentice-Hall.

Bullivant, B.M. (1984) *Pluralism: Cultural Maintenance and Evolution*. Clevedon, Avon: Multilingual Matters.

Children's Legal Centre (1983) 'Children's charters', *Childright* 1, 11–14.

Children's Legal Centre (1986) 'Rights of the child', *Childright* 32, 17–20.

Children's Legal Centre (1987) *Education Rights Handbook*. London: Children's Legal Centre.

Commission for Racial Equality (1978) *Books for Under Fives in Multi-Racial Britain*. London: Commission for Racial Equality.

Council for Education in World Citizenship (1980) *World Studies Resources Guide*. London: Council for Education in World Citizenship.

Council of Europe (1984) *Human Rights Education in Schools: Concepts, Attitudes and Skills*. Strasbourg: Council of Europe.

Council of Europe (1984) *The European Convention on Human Rights*. Strasbourg: Council of Europe.

Council on Interracial Books for Children, *Guidelines for Selecting Bias-Free Textbooks and Storybooks*. New York, n.d.

Craft, A. and Klein, G. (1986) *Agenda for Multicultural Teaching*. London: Longman (for the Schools Curriculum Development Committee).

Department of Education and Science (1977) *Education in Schools: A Consultative Document*. London: HMSO.

Department of Education and Science (1985) *The Curriculum from 5 to 16*. (Curriculum Matters 2.) London: HMSO.

Department of Education and Science (1988) *The Curriculum from 5 to 16*. (The Responses to Curriculum Matters 2.) London: Department of Education and Science.

Department of Education and Science, Assessment of Performance Unit (1988) *Attitudes and Gender Differences*. Windsor: NFER-Nelson.

Department of Education and Science, Assessment of Performance Unit (1988) *Pupils' Attitudes to Reading*. Windsor: NFER-Nelson.

Department of Education and Science, Assessment of Performance Unit (1988) *Pupils' Attitudes to Writing*. Windsor: NFER-Nelson.

Department of Education and Science, Assessment of Performance Unit (1988) *Science Progress Report 1977-8*. (List of Science Concepts and Knowledge.) London: Department of Education and Science.

Dunlop, J.P. (1983) *International and Multicultural Education Programme Working Papers*. Glasgow: Jordanhill College of Education.

Education in Human Rights Network (1987) *Bulletin No 1*. Scarborough: North Riding College.

Elkin, J. and Griffith, V. (eds) (1985) *Multi-racial Books for the Classroom*. Birmingham: Youth Libraries Group of the Library Association.

Elkin, J. and Triggs, P. (eds) (1986) *Childrens Books for a Multi-Cultural Society*. London: Books for Keeps.

Environmental Education Advisers Association (1981) *Environmental Education in the Curriculum*. Manchester: Manchester Local Education Authority Offices.

Fisher, S. and Hicks, D. (1982) *Planning and Teaching World Studies: An Interim Guide*. London: Schools Council.

Fisher, S. and Hicks, D. (1986) *World Studies 8-13: A Teachers Handbook*. Edinburgh and New York: Oliver & Boyd.

Frazer, M.J. and Kornhauser, A. (eds) (1986) *Ethics and Social Responsibility in Science Education*. Oxford: Pergamon Press.

Gage, N.L. (ed.) (1963) *Handbook of Research on Teaching*. Chicago: Rand McNally.

Gordon, M. (1964) *Assimilation in American Life: The Role of Race, Religion, and National Origins*. New York: Oxford University Press.

Grimshaw, J. (1986) *Feminist Philosophers*. Brighton: Wheatsheaf Books.

Independent Commission on International Development Issues (1980) *North–South: A Programme for Survival*. London: Pan Books.

Inner London Education Authority (1988) *Educational Material for a Multiethnic Society*. London: Inner London Education Authority.

International Association for the Study of Cooperation in Education (1988) 'Recent research in cooperative learning: implications for practitioners', *Newsletter* 9(3/4).

Jeffcoate, R. (1979) *Positive Image: Towards a Multiracial Curriculum*. London: Writers' and Readers' Publishing Co-operative.

Joyce, B. and Weil, M. (1986) *Models of Teaching*, 3rd edn. Englewood Cliffs, NJ: Prentice-Hall.

Kemmis, S. (1980) *The Action Research Planner*. Geelong: Deakin University Press.

Klein, G. (1985) *Reading into Racism*. London: Routledge.

Kohlberg, L., Levine, C. and Hewer, A. (1984) 'The current formulation of the theory', in L. Kohlberg (ed.), *Essays on Moral Development*, Vol. 2. San Francisco: Harper & Row.

Lewis, J. L. and Kelly, P. J. (eds) (1987) *Science and Technology Education and Future Human Needs*. Oxford: Pergamon Press.

Library Association, Youth Libraries Group (1985) *Multiracial Books for the Classroom*. London: Library Association.

Lynch, J. (1983) *The Multicultural Curriculum*. London: Batsford Academic.

Lynch, J. (1986) *Multicultural Education: Principles and Practice*. London: Routledge.

Lynch, J. (1989) *Multicultural Education in a Global Society*. London: Falmer Press.

Macdonald, B. (1975) *The Programme at Two*. Norwich: Centre for Applied Research in Education.

Manchester City Council Education Committee (1988) *Education for Peace in Manchester*. Manchester: Manchester Local Education Authority.

Marc Goldstein Memorial Trust (1988) *Teaching Resources for Education in International Understanding, Justice and Peace*, 2nd edn. London: University of London Institute of Education.

Michigan Department of Education (1979) *Bias Review Procedure*. Lancing, Michigan.

National Curriculum Council (1989) *A Framework for the Primary Curriculum*. (Curriculum Guidance Series No. 1.) York: National Curriculum Council.

National Curriculum Council (1989) *A Curriculum for All*. (Curriculum Guidance Series No. 2.) York: National Curriculum Council.

National Curriculum Council (1990) *Education for Economic and Industrial Understanding*. (Curriculum Guidance Series No. 4.) York: National Curriculum Council.

National Curriculum Council (1990) *Health Education*. (Curriculum Guidance Series No. 5.) York: National Curriculum Council.

National Curriculum Council (1990) *Careers Education and Guidance*. (Curriculum Guidance Series No. 6.) York: National Curriculum Council.

National Union of Teachers (1984) *Education for Peace*. London: National Union of Teachers.

National Youth Bureau (1988) *Social Education: Resources and Sources Information Pack*. Leicester: National Youth Bureau.

Oliver, H. (1987) *Sharing the World—A Prospect for Global Learning*. Toronto: Ontario Institute for Studies in Education.

Overseas Development Administration (1986) *Overseas Development and Aid*. London: Overseas Development Administration.

Parlett, M. and Hamilton, D. (1972) 'Evaluation as illumination', in D. Hamilton (ed.), *Beyond the Numbers Game*. London: Macmillan.

Perrott, E. (1982) *Effective Teaching*. Harmondsworth: Penguin.

Pike, G. and Selby, D. (1988) *Global Teacher, Global Learner*. London: Hodder & Stoughton.

Porter, N. and Taylor, N. (1972) *How to Assess the Moral Reasoning of Students*. Toronto: Ontario Institute for Studies in Education.

Ramsey, G. P. (1987) *Teaching and Learning in a Diverse World*. New York: Teachers' College, Columbia University.

Rao, A. N. (ed.) (1987) *Food, Agriculture and Education*. Oxford: Pergamon Press.

Schmuck, R. A., Runkel, J. P., Arends, J. H. and Arends, I. R. (1977) *The Second Handbook of Organization Development in Schools*. Palo Alto, CA: Mayfield.

Schneller, R. (1988) 'The Israeli experience of crosscultural misunderstanding: insights and lessons', in F. Poyatos (ed.), *Cross-cultural Perspectives in Nonverbal Communication*. Toronto: C. J. Hografe.

Schools Curriculum Development Committee/Law Society (1988) *Law in Education: News*, Summer.

Secretary of State for Education and Science (1985) *Report of the Committee of Enquiry into the Education of Children from Ethnic Minority Groups: Education for All* (The Swan Report.) London: HMSO.

Secretary of State of Canada (1987) *Canadian Multiculturalism Act*. Ottawa: House of Commons.

Sharan, S. (1984) *Cooperative Learning in the Classroom: Research in Desegregated Schools*. Hillsdale, NJ: Lawrence Erlbaum.

Sharan, S. (1989) 'Cooperative learning and helping behaviour in the multi-ethnic classroom', in H. Foot, M. Morgan and R. Shute (eds), *Children Helping Children*. London: John Wiley.

Sharan, S. and Shachar, H. (1988) *Language and Learning in the Cooperative Classroom*. New York: Springer-Verlag.

Simons, H. (ed.) (1988) *The National Curriculum*. Kendal: British Educational Research Association.

Southern Examination Group (1988) *Decision Making: Social and Life Skills*. Guildford: Southern Examination Group.

Speaker's Commission on Citizenship (1990) *Report: Encouraging Citizenship*. London: HMSO.

Stake, R. (1978) 'The case study method in social enquiry', *Educational Researcher* 7, 5–7.

Starkey, H. (1986) 'Human rights: the values for world studies and multicultural education', *Westminster Studies in Education* 9, 57–66.

Starkey, H. (1988) 'Practical activities for teaching and learning about human rights in schools'. Oxford: Westminster College. (Cyclo in draft form.)

Stenhouse, L. (1975) *An Introduction to Curriculum Research and Development*. London: Heinemann.

Taylor, C. (ed.) (1987) *Science Education and Information Transfer*. Oxford: Pergamon Press.

Tetreault, M.K.T. (1985) 'Feminist phase theory: an experience-derived evaluation model', *Journal of Higher Education* 56(4), 363–84.

The National Task Force on Citizenship Education (1977) *Education for Responsible Citizenship*. New York: McGraw-Hill.

Troyna, B. and Ball, W. (1985) 'Resistance rights and rituals: denominational schools and multi-cultural education', *Journal of Educational Policy* 2(1), 15–25.

United Kingdom Centre for European Education (1986) *Europe as a Resource for Education in International Understanding*. London: University of London Institute of Education.

United Nations (1978) *Human Rights: A Compilation of International Instruments*. New York: United Nations.

United Nations Educational, Scientific and Cultural Organization (1974) *Recommendation Concerning Education for International Understanding, Cooperation and Peace and Education Relating to Human Rights and Fundamental Freedoms*. Paris: UNESCO.

United Nations Scientific, Social and Cultural Organization (1977) *Environmental Education*. Paris: UNESCO.

United States Department of Justice (1987) *Law-related Education: Making a Difference*. Washington, DC.

United States Office of Educational Research and Improvement (1988) *Class Size and Public Policy: Politics and Panaceas*. Washington, DC.

Wallberg, H.J. (1984) 'Improving the productivity of America's schools', *Educational Leadership* 41(8), 19–27.

Westbrook, R.B. (1991) *John Dewey and American Democracy*. Ithaca, NY: Cornell University Press.

Whitehead, W. (1988) *Different Faces: Growing up with Books in a Multicultural Society*. London: Pluto Press.

Whitty, G. (1985) *Sociology and School Knowledge*. London: Methuen.

Wilson, D.C. (ed.) (1982) *Teaching Public Issues in a Canadian Context*. Toronto: Ontario Institute for Studies in Education.

Winter, R. (1986) 'Fictional critical writing', *Cambridge Journal of Education* 16(3), 175–83.

Yaakobi, D. and Sharan, S. (1985) 'Teacher beliefs and practices: the discipline carries the message', *Journal of Education for Teaching* 11(2), 187–99.

Name Index

Subject Index